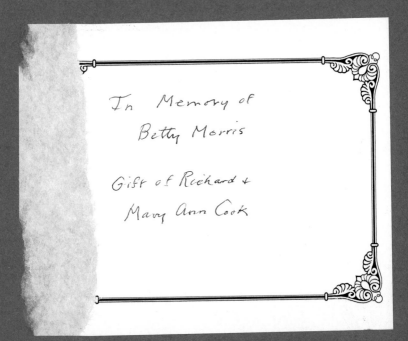

 Bears

# Bears

A BRIEF HISTORY

Bernd Brunner

*Translated from the German by Lori Lantz*

yale university press    *new haven and london*

Published with assistance from the foundation established in memory of Philip Hamilton McMillan of the Class of 1894, Yale College.

Designed by Sonia L. Shannon
Set in Stempel Schneidler type by The Composing Room of Michigan, Inc.
Printed in the United States of America.

Library of Congress Cataloging-in-Publication Data
Brunner, Bernd, 1964–
[Eine kurze Geschichte der Bären. English]
Bears : a brief history / Bernd Brunner ; translated from the German by Lori Lantz.
p. cm.
Includes bibliographical references and index.
ISBN 978-0-300-12299-2 (hardcover : alk. paper)
1. Bears—History.   I. Title.
QL737.C27B78 2007
599.78—dc22
2007021322

A catalogue record for this book is available from the British Library.

The paper in this book meets the guidelines for permanence and durability of the Committee on Production Guidelines for Book Longevity of the Council on Library Resources.

10 9 8 7 6 5 4 3 2 1

# Contents

# Bears

# Introduction

What might the first encounter between human and bear have been like? Perhaps a prehistoric hunter watched from his hiding place as a bear stood up on its hind legs. What other animal had he ever seen stand erect? Other than bears, only a few types of rodents and—oddly enough—owls stand upright as humans do. Our ancient observer was probably also amazed by how dexterously the bear could reach for fruit with its forepaws. He could have noticed how the bear's paws differ from his own hands: since the bear has no thumbs, each paw's five "fingers" possesses equal importance. Despite its large nose, the bear's face, with his eyes aligned in a nearly frontal plane, would also have seemed familiar. Since its feet seem almost humanlike as well, the hunter would have realized which animal had produced the tracks he had seen earlier in the forest. And he may have drawn the comparison between the bear's long claws and his own fingernails. Once he had killed and skinned the animal and had seen how slim and light-colored its body was under its fur, the hunter would certainly have recognized how much the bear resembled him.

As early humans became more familiar with bears, they may have realized that the animals

Norwegian Bear, by Etienne Geoffroy Saint-Hilaire (1824).

ate the same things they did: whether the herbs and berries that they plucked, the roots that they dug from the ground, the gophers and other small animals that they hunted, or the fish that they caught. A bear may even have guided them to sources of honey. On occasion, humans and bears also surely came into conflict over their choice of caves. Over time, ancient people began to perceive bears in two ways: as intimately related to them, but also as serious competitors. In the long run, humans were the victors, even though they possessed only primitive weapons and their opponents were considerably stronger. They pushed their way farther and farther into the bears' territory and drove the shy animals out, felling entire forests to clear the land for planting.

In both Eurasia and North America, the bear occupied a prominent and unique place in early cultures and had a special relationship to humans. Wherever people and bears lived in proximity, humans displayed the same ambivalent behavior: although the bears were driven out, hunted, and killed, their relative resemblance to humans

Auf der Bärenjagd.

and their enormous strength commanded our respect. This paradox formed the cornerstone of *Bear Ceremonialism in the Northern Hemisphere,* a study published by American cultural anthropologist Irving Hallowell in 1926. Although the festivals celebrated by both Eurasian peoples and many Native American tribes varied from region to region, Hallowell found that they shared the same basic impetus: the bear was honored as the lord of the forest or the son of the supreme ruler, whose calling it was to uphold justice. Groups that were widely separated geographically, Hal-

Early bear hunt in Germania.

lowell claimed, shared the belief that a bear killed in the hunt would enter a new life.

Even the similarity of the euphemisms used in various cultures to refer to bears—referring to the word "bear" itself was often thought to be tempting fate and was therefore taboo—demonstrates that the animal occupied a comparable role in all of them. According to Holloway, the bear was called "cousin" by the Abenaki, Tsimshian, and Tahltan Indians; "grandfather" by the Penobscot; and "four-legged human" or "chief's son" by the Plains Cree. The Siberian Kets endowed him with noble names such as "fur father," "old claw man," or "beautiful animal." The Samoyeds, also from Siberia, called him "old father," while the Estonians named him "broadfoot," and the Carpathian Huzuls referred to him as "little uncle" or "great hairy one." Finally, the Laplanders dubbed the bear "the old man with the fur garment," while their Swedish neighbors used the names "old man," "gold feet," or "twelve men's strength." If these aliases sound romantic to us today, we need to keep in mind that they reflected a completely different relation to the animal kingdom, one in which the bear represented the single large animal that resembled, and competed with, humans. The existence of apes, let alone their close genetic relationship with us, was unknown in the Northern Hemisphere.

THIS BOOK EXAMINES the shared history of humans and bears. This history is composed of many stories—some of them recorded, some of them lost, and some of them told and retold so many times that boundaries between fact and fiction have become blurred, making it difficult or impossible to untangle the two. The relations between humans and bears throughout history are complex because they play out within the poles of attraction and repulsion, combining these seemingly irreconcilable opposites in almost every possible way. In other words, our interactions with bears are laden with mixed feelings: our forebears venerated, killed, caressed, tortured, nurtured, ate, respected, and despised them. In some instances, these paradoxical attitudes can even be found within the framework of a single culture. In comparatively recent times, humans have also begun to scrutinize bears closely out of scientific interest. It may often seem that this rational outlook has completely replaced our forefathers' more emotional or even spiritual views of bears. A return to older worldviews may not be possible or even desirable, but, if we look more closely, we will see that bears continue to exert a powerful and seemingly inexplicable fascination for us.

Writing about bears, however, is a dangerous business. The existence of so many pleasurable accounts of bears can easily blind us to the importance of those that are less so. And it can seem as though everybody is reading over your shoulder: teddy bear lovers, biologists, hunters, poachers, animal-rights advocates, and others, all of whom—in one way or another—have a stake in bears and bring their own perspective and history to the subject. Rather than try to single out the "correct" perspective on bears, I trace these interwoven strands by focusing where cultural and natural history intersect. I will tell some of the stories of humans and bears and explore certain key topics and questions. A number of the examples I provide along the way are drawn from outside the borders of the English-speaking world. While the saga of bears in America plays an important role in this book, the tangled histories of bears in places like Russia or Japan are equally fascinating and deserve our attention. At the same time, the complexity of the subject means that no book about bears can hope to be comprehensive. However, I want to provide a sense of the scope of these remarkable animals—the many varieties and their habitats and behaviors summarized by the misleadingly simple term "bear."

Despite their diversity and illustrious history, the state of bears today is sobering. These once abundant animals are now largely confined to areas with little or no human civilization. Is it possible for humans and bears to share the same space at all? Why is it so hard for us to imagine these extraordinary creatures clearly without caricatures immediately filling our minds? Do we really know what bears are like, what they feel? Do bears deserve their reputation as particularly dangerous predators? And, if so, who is actually preying on whom these days?

Bears are strong, intelligent, and fascinating

animals whose ways deserve respect. Examining our dealings with bears throughout history will improve our understanding of our relationship to them today. What other animal occupies as much space in the human imagination as the bear? Bears are present in our entertainment and advertising, in our art and literature, in our folk wisdom and popular sayings. Although bears have disappeared from vast stretches of the earth, they continue to populate our personal and collective dreams.

# Der braune Bär.

Pl. 46.

Lith.qy. bei I Crebesar Selia.

# Der weisse Bär.

# CHAPTER ONE

# Tracking the Paths of Bears

Most scientists today recognize eight species of bears worldwide. The brown bear *(Ursus arctos)* is identifiable by its furry coat of blond, brown, or even black hair—sometimes with silver tips— and by a large hump of muscle above its shoulders. It is the most widely distributed bear in the Northern Hemisphere. The polar bear *(Ursus maritimus)* lives in and around the Arctic and has white or cream-colored fur and a thick layer of blubber to protect it from the cold. The much smaller American black bear *(Ursus americanus),* or baribal, is the most common bear species in North America. In contrast, the spectacled bear *(Tremarctos ornatus)* lives only in the Andes tropical basin. Its name derives from the distinctive light markings across its face. These light patterns can also appear on the animal's chest, making the spectacled bear only one of several types of bears with distinctive markings there. The Asian black bear *(Ursus thibetanus),* which can be found along a line that stretches from Iran to Japan, sports a large, white crescent. The sloth bear *(Melursus ursinus),* which inhabits southern Asia, has long fur and a white, V-shaped mark. Thanks to long, curved claws and a specially shaped mouth that enables it to eat insects, the sloth bear was indeed first mistakenly identified

When classification was simple: brown bear and white bear.

as a giant sloth. The sun bear *(Helarctos malay-anus),* with its short, sleek fur and a yellow marking in the shape of a horseshoe, is the smallest member of the bear family and lives in the tropical rainforests of Southeast Asia. Finally, the great panda *(Ailuropoda melanoleuca),* a native of central and southern China, has a distinctive black-and-white coat. He is most different from all other modern bear species.

ALL BEARS LIVING TODAY have descended from a common ancestor known as *Ursavus,* or "dawn bear." This animal, which lived about twenty million years ago, was about the size of a small terrier. Even at this early point in evolutionary history, however, *Ursavus* had a jaw already markedly different from that of a dog. Over time, groups of this early bear species split off and wandered into different habitats, where they adapted to new and better environments and to available sources of food. Each group underwent its own course of evolution.

One of the earliest to evolve from one of these groups—about ten million years ago—was the giant panda, while another group ultimately produced the spectacled bear (which arrived in South America long before the brown and black bear). Several million years later, during the Pliocene, a bear known as *Ursus minimus* first appeared. Before this ancestral bear further evolved into *Ursus etruscus,* additional groups split off and ultimately became the American black bear, the Asian black bear, the sloth bear, and the sun bear.

*Ursus etruscus,* however, which lived about one and a half million years ago, was the progenitor of both the cave bear and other bears that would become the brown bear and the polar bear. This bear migrated from Europe deep into Asia. The mighty cave bear, an ursine giant that shared the earth with early humans, disappeared only about ten to twenty thousand years ago. Polar bears, in turn, are considered to be the youngest bears of all. Scientists long believed that brown and polar bears evolved at widely different times, but genetic analysis has since demonstrated that the two are close relatives: between two and three hundred thousand years ago, the first polar bears evolved from North American brown bears.

ALTHOUGH TO US THE concept of "bear" seems self-explanatory, the search to identify exactly what it is that makes a bear part of a particular group (and what distinguishes each one from the others) constitutes a long and convoluted chapter in the history of science. Of course, this quest to categorize the bear species is also part of the history we share with these animals. Aristotle (384–322 B.C.), the first thinker to attempt to classify the animal kingdom, conducted his research by questioning hunters, fishermen, sailors, shepherds, and farmers about animals they had seen. While he founded the discipline of taxonomy with his resulting work, *History of Animals,* his classification system was rudimentary. He divided the animals into those with and without blood, corresponding to our distinction between vertebrates and invertebrates. Bears belonged to the first group, of course, and to the "viviparous quadrupeds," or mammals, but Aristotle, who probably knew only the brown bear, did not further subdivide this category into different types. Such distinctions did not emerge until bears from other countries and continents became known to scientists in the course of the great voyages of discovery. However, this diversity sowed considerable confusion. Who could possibly have the perspective and authority necessary to distinguish between different groups of bears?

Throughout human history, each scientist could base his classification scheme only on the limited knowledge he possessed at a particular point in time. Albertus Magnus (1200–1280) recognized three kinds of bears: black, brown, and white. Conrad Gessner (1516–1565) introduced a division encompassing "primary bears" and "stone bears." Johann Elias Ridiger (1695–1767), a

German painter of animals known for his precision, took a completely novel approach by claiming that all differences in the appearance of bears were due solely to the animals' ages.

The great French naturalist Georges-Louis Leclerc, Comte de Buffon (1707–1788), in turn, was more specific in that he distinguished between a brown bear; a black bear, *Ursus americanus;* and two white varieties, *ours blanc terrestre* and *ours blanc maritime*—in other words, the polar bear. Carolus Linnaeus (1707–1778), the "father of taxonomy," recognized only the varieties *Ursus arctos* and *Ursus maritimus.* These examples merely illustrate the range of creative solutions scientists proposed to this taxonomic puzzle. For the German-Russian biologist Carl Grevé, who wrote a historical overview of bear classification just a few years before the dawn of the twentieth century, the time must have seemed ripe for sweeping away the past confusion and organizing the bears once and for all. He decided that none of the bears he had ever seen in the wild or in a zoo resembled one another, and he therefore proposed that all bears in Europe and northern Asia should belong to a single group—namely *Ursus arctos.* The many different kinds of bears that existed in this extensive region, he argued, were thus not genuinely distinct varieties but merely "local breeds."

One notable type of bear that features only briefly in Grevé's account is the grizzly. Grevé obviously didn't know that the grizzly's monstrous image had already been canonized in the zoological nomenclature by the naturalist George Ord in 1815, when he named the animal *Ursus horribilis* or even, in some instances, *Ursus horribilis horribilis.* Such a negative assessment in a taxonomic name was unusual, to say the least. This gap in the scientific knowledge about the species was later filled to overflowing by the mammal specialist Clinton (C.) Hart Merriam (1855–1942), who in the early twentieth century dedicated many years to working out a hairsplitting scheme to classify grizzlies.

Armed with a magnifying glass, he painstakingly investigated every bear tooth and skull in the Museum of Natural History in Washington, D.C. Merriam proceeded to subdivide *Ursus horribilis* into no less than eighty-six separate subspecies, from the Absaroka grizzly *(Ursus absarokus),* found in Montana, to the Yellowstone Park grizzly *(Ursus mirus),* from Wyoming. As these names suggest, Merriam's designations generally indicate the regions in which the bears lived. He saw nothing grotesque in proposing such a vast number of subspecies and firmly believed that "it is not the business of the naturalist to either create or suppress species, but to endeavor to ascertain how many Nature has established." Merriam's classification scheme, however, has not withstood the test of time; it has come to be recognized as a classic example of taxonomic oversplitting. Today, the names *Ursus horribilis* and *Ursus arctos horribilis* are used only rarely; they remind us of how this animal was demonized and driven to extinction in many parts of North

Ursavus may have looked like this.

America. More recent classifications based on genetic analysis distinguish between two and seven subspecies of North American brown bears based on different body size, skull structure, and fur color. An example is the concept of three evolutionary significant units (ESUs) for North American brown bears—with implications for conservation and management to preserve the evolutionary history of the clades.

LET US RETURN TO THE giant panda, an animal that proved to be exceptionally difficult to classify. The species long remained somewhat unanchored between the great and small bears and was classified with its cousins, the much smaller, raccoonlike red pandas. At first glance, pandas resemble the great bears due to their size, but their skull is shaped like that of a raccoon, as are their jaws. The sounds pandas produce can be best described as hissing or bleating and have nothing in common with the brown bear's roar. In terms of evolutionary history, pandas are also the most distant relatives in the great bear family. Despite these factors, zoologists classify pandas as great bears, primarily because of their genetic characteristics.

IN OUR TIME, IT HAS often been the sad duty of scientists to document the disappearance of species, but the theory of evolution teaches that new ones can also arise. Could these developmental processes bring a new kind of bear into being? In the first edition of his epochal work *On the Origin of Species,* Charles Darwin speculated that bears could one day evolve into completely aquatic creatures. Darwin based this remarkable hypothesis on a comment by the Arctic explorer Samuel Hearne, who traveled Canada's western coast at the end of the eighteenth century. Hearne reported how the region's black bears managed to find a meal in the early summer, before the berries had ripened in the forest: they would swim along the surface of the water with their mouths wide open and swallow the insects floating there in great numbers. Assuming the insect population remained constant, and no other animals were better suited to skimming them, Darwin argued, "I can see no difficulty in a race of bears being rendered, by natural selection, more and more aquatic in their structure and habits, with larger and larger mouths, till a creature was produced as monstrous as a whale." The father of evolution is said to have later bitterly regretted this flight of fancy. But is the idea of largely aquatic bears as unlikely as it seems? As the winters get shorter and the polar ice melts faster every year, polar bears will have to get used to spending more time in the water than on the ice shelf. But given the speed at which the environment is changing, it is uncertain whether the animals will be able to adapt fast enough.

Even if giant bear-whales are an unlikely development, bear evolution seems well under way. It has long been known that a grizzly and a polar bear can produce offspring—such crossbreeding has successfully occurred in zoos. The Department of the Environment and Natural Resources for Canada's Northwest Territories nevertheless took the scientific community by surprise when it announced in early 2006 that a hunter had killed a bear that was a cross between a grizzly and a polar bear in the Canadian Arctic. The bear had the grizzly's characteristic humped back and long claws, and its fur was neither pure nor yellowish-white like a polar bear's, but rather light brown. Hunter Jim Martell, who had a permit to shoot a polar bear, was surprised (and presumably concerned) by the bear's appearance. A genetic test proved that he had bagged the offspring of a polar bear and a grizzly. The existence of such a hybrid bear in the wild was especially surprising since both species tend to react very aggressively toward each other. Such an encounter would more likely result in a fight than in a mixed-breed bear.

# CHAPTER TWO

# Transformations

The almost tender names for bears collected by Irving Hallowell demonstrate that humans once considered themselves linked with bears (as well as with many other animals) in ways that today seem mysterious. For us, our ancestors' apparent connection to nature easily leads to all kinds of fanciful speculation about their interaction with individual animal species. Of course, many myths reinforce the impression that bears played an important role in the mental and spiritual life of early humans. But we should remember that these stories have been handed down over the course of millennia and certainly have undergone a number of changes in the process. Whatever the original form of these myths, it is clear that a worldview that considered humans to be one with nature is a thing of the past. Science's progressive demystification of nature—a phenomenon of the last few hundred years—is partly responsible, but Christianity played an even greater role by driving out the old nature religions of pagan peoples.

As the animal that, perhaps more than any other, embodied the pagan concept of a kinship between man and nature, the bear played a key role in early Christian legends. Saint Ursula, for example, received her name because she successfully defended eleven thousand virgins against

Bear's Belly. Arikara. Photographed by Edward S. Curtis in 1908. A member of the medicine fraternity, wrapped in his sacred bearskin.

bears—a feat that could represent the saving of these Christian innocents from the dangers of nature worship. Other saints, such as the missionary Korbinian, demonstrated their power by taming bears. After a wild bear killed his horse during a pilgrimage to Rome, the saint loaded his possessions on the bear's back as punishment and continued on his way. Once he reached Rome, the holy man released the bear from its servitude.

THE MANY SURVIVING stories about bears reveal the variety of roles that they have played in the human imagination, from enemies of mankind to their protective spirits. One of the most prominent and persistent threads of such tales is the assumption that bears and humans are intimately related. While this kinship sometimes appears to be merely symbolic, at other times one can sense a genuine belief underlying such accounts that bears are our not-so-distant relatives. From our modern perspective, of course, this distinction belongs to the apes. But when we realize that most peoples in the Northern Hemisphere have known of the existence of apes only for the past few centuries, we should not be surprised that many legends and myths speculate about a bear-human connection. Of all the animals early Eurasians and Americans could encounter, it was the bear that most closely resembled a human being. And the physical similarities seem to be the reason why humans have often considered the boundary between themselves and bears to be remarkably permeable.

One such story was handed down from ancient Greece, where female bears served as symbols of motherhood. The beautiful nymph Callisto had broken her vow of chastity to become one of the many lovers of Zeus. She became pregnant as a result of her liaison, and when her condition became apparent the furious Artemis, the goddess of the hunt, turned Callisto into a bear. In spite of her new form, Callisto gave birth to a human son, Arcas, who grew up separated from his mother. Years later, while hunting, Arcas happened upon the bear Callisto, whom he of course did not recognize as his mother. As her son took aim, Zeus decided to rescue Callisto and set her forever in the sky, where she is still visible as the "Big Dipper," the constellation known in much of the world as the "Great Bear." Zeus's illegitimate son Arcas, in turn, can be seen as the particularly bright star "Arcturus," which can be found by extending the line formed by the Great Bear's tail.

The tendency to anthropomorphize bears was particularly strong among the Native Americans. The Cherokee, who originally lived in the region between the Ohio River and what is now Georgia and Alabama, believed that bears were transformed humans. They were convinced that at one time some of their forefathers had traded their difficult human lives for the more carefree lot of bears, and that they and bears thus shared the same ancestors. This kinship, however, did not prevent the Cherokee from hunting bears— which they accomplished wearing wooden masks and bear fur, in order to be able to draw nearer to their prey. The Kiowa, who lived in the West

Callisto's hand transforms into a bear paw.

and, later, the Southwest, likewise considered bears to be their forefathers. Despite this familial standing, however, they greatly feared the animals and believed that their destructive power meant even medicine men were not safe from them. The Ojibway Indians of the Great Lakes region, in contrast, considered bears—which they viewed as descended from humans—to be sacred. For them, bears were medicine men who were the messengers of immortal life. At the same time, they also believed that when a bear attacked one of its own kind, the attacking bear was actually a transformed human being. If the victim of such an attack succeeded in touching or injuring the so-called bearwalker, his foe would revert to his human form and die.

For the southwestern Yavapi, in what is now Arizona, the only difference between men and bears was the fact that humans could make fire. For this reason they did not hunt bears, and the

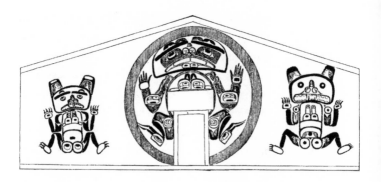

animals could supposedly be found living in the immediate vicinity of the tribe's settlements as a result. The situation was similar among the Pueblo: their rule against eating one's own kind also made bear meat taboo. The northwestern Tlingit believed that a woman had once married a grizzly bear and had two children by him. They thus avoided harming grizzlies, although they did hunt black bears.

Bear symbols on houses of the Kwakiutl Indians in the Pacific Northwest.

Various Native American tribes had bear clans that entertained mystical relations with the animal and even identified with it as their totem. As David Rockwell explains, members of the Bear Clan of the Yuchi Indians, in what is now the southeastern United States, claimed to be descended from the bear, and they prayed to the animal and danced in its honor at a New Year's ceremony.

Many tribes believed that bears could transform into humans, other animals, or even objects. In an ethnographic survey of the southern Yukon Territory, Catharine McClellan noted that, according to the Tlingit, "people must always speak carefully of them, since bears (no matter how far away) have the power to hear human speech. Even though a person murmurs a few careless words, the bear will take revenge." Tlingit shamans also had special songs to express their oneness with the grizzly and were even thought to be able to change into bears themselves.

The idea that people were related to bears played an important role not only in North America, but in Europe and Asia as well. A saga from northern Russia relates that the first bear was the product of a relationship between a forest spirit and a woman who was half-human and half-animal. Centuries-old legends of the west Siberian Kets and Voguls also reveal a variety of theories about the bear's origin: in some accounts, the bear's ancestors are humans, while in others he is descended from heroes and female forest spirits or, conversely, from heroes' daughters and male spirits. Some stories claim that the first bear's parents were a man who had been cursed by his mother and a hero's daughter who had been turned into a female bear.

In some tales, humans became bears as a result of unfortunate tree-climbing episodes. In one account, a man loses his way in the forest. When he climbs a moss-covered tree, his body becomes overgrown with moss, too, and he turns into a bear. In a Ket legend, in turn, a man undresses himself in the forest and climbs up a tree. Meanwhile, someone steals his clothes and he subsequently grows a bear's pelt. Although he looked like a bear from then on, the story concludes, he could still understand human language.

Other stories about bearlike humans come from Scandinavia. Legends relate that after the founding of the Norwegian kingdom more than a thousand years ago, an army of especially strong men was called into being. These fearsome warriors, or "berserkers," dedicated their lives to the supreme god Wotan, also known as Odin. The word "berserker" is presumably a combination of "beri," Old Norse for "bear," and "serkr," for "shirt," and thus literally means "clothed as a bear." According to ancient Germanic texts, berserkers were indistinguishable from ordinary men under normal conditions, but when aroused they could perform incredible feats such as ripping the rim of a shield with their teeth, swallowing glowing coals, or walking through blazing fire. *Heidrek's Saga* relates that the twelve berserkers who were the brothers and sons of Arngrim of Holm possessed swords, forged by dwarves, that they wielded not only in battle but also, apparently in the grip of delusions, against trees and rocks.

An ordinary mortal had little chance when faced with an angry berserker, but there was a way to prevent the worst: before an outburst, a berserker would briefly become drowsy, providing a momentary opportunity to tie him up. A variety of triggers could prompt a berserker to "go berserk," including the approach of darkness, strong emotions such as wrath or belligerence, intense pain, the taste of raw meat, or, in the case of the Icelander Odd, the sight of blood. After his father and his brother were killed by a polar bear, Odd beat the beast to death. From this point on,

Odd was a classic berserker: irascible, unsociable, and tremendously strong. Another legend relates that a seer once observed the berserkers Dufthak and Storolf as they fought at sundown in the forms of a bear and a bull. The next morning a desolate crater marked the location of their struggle. The sagas are largely forgotten today, but the figure of the berserker still provides a popular blueprint for comics and video games.

As late as the eleventh century, there were still aristocrats who considered themselves to be descended from bears. Two examples are Earl Siward of Northumberland, who died in 1055, and the Danish king Svend Estridsen (1047–1074). Siward's father was even said to have had ears like those of a bear.

Bears also played a prominent role in the cultural imagination of the gypsies, as we see in the following legend: "One day a young woman realized that she must be pregnant even though she had never been close to a man. In her shame she decided to throw herself into the river. But the closer she came to the water the more it drew away from her. Then a man came up to her out of the river and said, 'Do not be ashamed, for you will bring forth an animal that is capable of working like a man.' When she came home, the virgin gave birth to a bear, and as he grew up the gypsies taught him to dance and perform comical movements. Since that time men and bears have traveled together as entertainers through the world."

In addition to suggesting that humans are descended from bears or vice versa, mythology and

Bearlike boy (fourteenth century).

folklore offer a number of stories in which humans, while not actually related to bears, are adopted and raised by them. Similar accounts of feral children can be found around the globe. Whether their foster parents were supposedly wolves in the Indian jungle, apes in Uganda, or wild dogs in Russia, the mixture of disgust and curiosity that the fate of such children evokes ensures that their stories have found their way into numerous travel books.

Johann Daniel Geyer, for example, wrote about the "bear people" of Lithuania in his 1735 essay "Pleasant Thoughts for Indolent Traveling Hours." He reported having seen a "creature" in that country who lived among nuns and who was put to work carrying water and wood. Although she looked like a human, she would drop whatever she was carrying whenever she caught sight of a tame bear and run toward the animal on all fours to play. Geyer further claimed to have encountered another "bear person" in a vast forest. In this case, the man's bearish nature manifested itself in a preference for raw meat, honey, and fruit, as well as in the habit of walking on all fours instead of upright.

In the second half of the seventeenth century Bernard Connor, an Irishman who served as a doctor to the king of Poland, reported a similar story about a twelve-year-old boy found in a German forest and brought to Warsaw. Connor wrote that the child, who emitted bearlike noises, could approach bears without fear. The animals, in turn, did not harm him—presumably because they recognized him as their ward. At first his fellow humans pitied the boy and treated him as less than human, but once they realized how close his relationship was to the bears they began to respect him as a mythical being.

Some Turks claimed that they saw four bear-people deep in a forest in the late 1930s and that they captured three of them. The beings were naked, and their entire bodies were covered with hair so that only their faces revealed their human descent. Eight years earlier in the same area, a farm woman carrying her child on her back was attacked by a female bear as she collected fire-wood. As she fled, she lost her son, not quite a year old. After the bear-people were spotted, people assumed that one of them was the missing boy and that the bear had suckled and protected him as he was growing up.

Despite the prevalence and appeal of such tales, it would be close to impossible for an animal even to physically carry a child. Unlike a dog pup or a wolf or bear cub, a human baby is not programmed to freeze in an adult animal's jaws —on the contrary, it would struggle mightily. The belief that children could be raised by wild animals could, however, have been encouraged by the fact that some animal mothers do nurse the young of other species. This behavior has often been exploited in zoos: if a female bear proved to be a threat to her offspring, for example, the cubs would be taken from her and placed in a basket with a mother dog. In fact, dogs have been known to accept not only bears but also young lions, tigers, and cats as "adoptive" children.

Bear nursing her two cubs and a human (1605).

In the fairy tales of many cultures, in turn, male bears are sometimes featured as seducers of women—an image at odds with their frequent portrayal as loners and misanthropes. The most famous of these tales is the story known in various Romance languages as "Jean de l'Ours," "Juan del Oso," or "Gian dell'Orso." Regardless of his nationality, the title character—a bear, of course—kidnaps a girl or a young woman and then successfully wins her favor. The resulting child is as strong as his animal father and as intelligent as his human mother. In the stories that follow this pattern, this unusual child has a name that reveals his ursine origins: Bearsson, Hans Bear, Little Bearhans, Peter Bear, Martis the Bear, or Bearsear. In the better-known tale "Snow

White and Rose Red," discussed in the chapter "Bear Substitutes," the animal bridegroom also appears in the form of a bear.

In other stories, it is only after she is married that the bear's bride discovers her husband's animal nature. An old legend of the Finno-Ugric Votyaks describes the ill-fated marriage of a famous magician. One night the magician began to groan like a bear in his sleep. "Why are you groaning?" his wife asks. "It's nothing," he answers. "I'm going to walk up and down in the courtyard, and then it will stop." On his way out, he somewhat curiously sheds his clothes and leaves them in the pantry. His wife, who has slipped out quietly after him, sees him go naked into the woods, clamber up a rowan tree, and turn into a bear. He then comes back from the forest and goes into the village to cast his spells. His wife

runs terrified back to the house and hides in the pantry. After a while the bear returns. Unable to find his robe, he knocks on the door and asked for his clothes. His bear's voice so frightens his wife that she cannot utter a word. Finally the magician bellows and returns to the forest, trapped in bear form for the rest of his days.

During the Renaissance, people were preoccupied with the "animal within" and the possibility that humans could slip into animal form. Animal masks were highly popular even though—or perhaps because—they were condemned by moralists. Such masks offered a way to violate the natural dividing line between humans and animals and even celebrate this play with sacrosanct boundaries. Later, ordinary people would transform into bears—at least symbolically—for the spring festivals in western and central Europe. In many places, the Carnival bear, a man in a suit of dried pea husks, would parade to music through the streets between Transfiguration Sunday and Ash Wednesday. The "bear" and his companions collected money that the revelers later spent together at the tavern. The ritual symbolized the coming of spring, since the power of winter, which the bear represented, could be broken by driving the bears from their dens and forcing the peas out of their pods.

In the high mountains boys or men dressed as bears, using straw to emulate fir. They would let the straw be plucked to lay in the hen's nests or under brood geese in order to encourage the poultry to lay eggs. A similar figure existed in

Transformed prince and his beloved (1911).

Silesia, now a part of Poland: there a man whose legs were wrapped in straw would be accompanied by young bears on his left and right. The yearly awakening of nature in Switzerland was heralded in turn by the "May bear," a four-foot-high, beehive-shaped construction woven from the first green twigs and decorated with flowers and colored ribbons. Powered by a person concealed beneath it, this vegetation demon would run through the streets of Swiss villages, followed by children sounding bells and gongs.

If we are tempted to smile at the seemingly quaint beliefs of earlier generations, we should remember that some people today still believe that half-human, half-bear creatures walk the earth. The mysterious "snow men," or Yeti, of the Himalayas continue to fire imaginations not only in Nepal, but around the world. According to popular accounts, the Yeti have prominent eyebrows and long hair, they generally walk upright, and they live among the rocky cliffs in the mountains, which are of course conveniently riddled with

Costumed man in an Eastern European bear festival.

Straw bear at carnival time (Germany, late nineteenth century).

caves. Of the two types of Yeti that are distinguished by the Nepalese, the "Chuktey" is considered to be less aggressive than the "Mhetey." If we consider how much these creatures are said to resemble people, it should not be much of a surprise that the word *mhe* means "human" in the language of the Gurung, one of Nepal's ethnic groups. According to local stories, a Mhetey even once kidnapped a healer to try to cure others of his kind who were sick. The Nepalese themselves, however, believe that Yeti are simply bears, as does the Japanese researcher Matako Nabuka, who claims to have observed the "snow

people" in Nepal, Tibet, and Bhutan for twelve years. And the Tyrolean mountaineer Reinhold Messner once came across a stuffed Himalayan bear that was being displayed as a "Yeti," which gives this theory even more weight.

However, Nabuka's countryman Yoshiteru Takahashi, a cryptozoologist (natural scientist specializing in hypothetical species), does not let this view bother him at all. He is convinced that the Yeti are beings distinct from both humans and bears and tirelessly continues his search for them in the Himalayas, equipped with temperature-sensitive infrared cameras and movement alarms. He claims to have seen suspicious footprints repeatedly. Unfortunately, his camera has failed him on every occasion that he has stood face to face with a snow man.

# CHAPTER THREE

# The Mystery of the Cave Bear

Let us return to our imagined scene in which an early human sees a bear for the first time. What kind of bear played the starring role in this opening episode of the long drama between bears and men? We will never know for sure, but it may have been a cave bear. The last cave bear lived more than ten thousand years ago, but questions about these extinct giants have fascinated researchers for the past two hundred years. What relationship existed between cave bears and humans? Were the lives of cave bears actually intertwined with those of humans—as some evidence seems to suggest—and, if so, did the bears serve as competitors, or as prey, or as figures revered by a widespread cult? And what caused these mighty animals to disappear completely?

When the German pastor Johann Friedrich Esper published his 1774 book on "newly discovered zoolites of unknown four-footed animals," scientists throughout Europe became interested in the large bones that recently had been found in caves located in a mountainous region in Franconia, in southeastern Germany. Initially, the scientists' imaginations knew no bounds, and they seriously debated whether the bones could have come from unicorns or even from dragons. Esper compared the bones with those of other mam-

A vision of the Stone Age from around 1890.

mal species and came to the conclusion that "these creatures indisputably do not belong to the family of primates." "Apes are thus impossible," he continued, adding that "the six or seven molars possessed by dogs and their relatives, wolves and hyenas, utterly rule out these animals." Furthermore, "from the race of cats neither lions, nor tigers, nor leopards bear any resemblance." Through this process of elimination the thorough researcher finally concluded that "only the bears merit longer consideration."

His analysis was farsighted, but many questions remained. The bones of the "unknown creature," which seemed to be unusually large, could not be classified as those of brown bears. Esper believed that they were more likely polar bears, but somehow they did not fit the picture, either. Another twenty years passed before Johann Christian Rosenmüller, who also investigated the bones, designated a new subspecies for them. He dubbed the animal *Ursus spelaeus,* or "cave bear," and, following convention, completed this designation by adding his own name. Thus *Ursus spelaeus rosenmüller* entered the scientific literature.

Rosenmüller, actually an anatomy professor at the University of Leipzig, devoted every free moment to his real passion: researching caves. He believed that caves "penetrated and undermined the entire surface of the planet" and imagined them to be "the earth's entrails." His 1805 book on "remarkable caves" brought a number of hidden places from Portugal to Siberia to the metaphorical light of day. In caves, Rosenmüller wrote, "We become aware of thousands of objects that, partly due to their deceptive similarity to works of art and partly to their own sublime organization, demand our entire attention." With the fascination of the truly obsessed, he saw the objects of his study as full of portentous secret meaning. "It is therefore forgivable," he continued, "if—here in these eerie vaults near the bones of forgotten creatures, where eternal night and deathly silence hold sway—we, torn from the kingdom of the living, give ourselves over to the pictures of our imaginations and believe ourselves to be standing at the portals of eternity and Elysium until other demands, and perhaps fear and horror, drive us away from these objects once again." While this otherworldly vision may seem overwrought to us, Rosenmüller's views of caves formed the groundwork for future scientific thought in this area.

But why did bears—which are presumably less susceptible to flights of subterranean fancy— seek out such caves, apparently in large groups at that? Some of Rosenmüller's contemporaries believed that rising waters forced the animals to retreat into the caverns. The coating of clay found on the bones seemed to support this hypothesis. Esper himself had assumed that "a violent occurrence" such as "floods rising from the depths" or "the ocean spilling out of its bounds" had likely driven the animals together. "Experience continues to teach us that the wildest of beasts gather together during natural catastrophes in order to

The Gailenreuth bone cave.

try to save themselves," he claimed. "Their calls to one another and some unidentifiable instinct infallibly drive the creatures of one race or species to join the others of its kind."

Rosenmüller did away with such sensational theories, claiming that the bears had simply sought shelter in the caves. However, the fossil discoveries fired his imagination in a different direction, as his reaction to studies of the "remarkable bone caves" of Egypt shows. "If 100,000 dog skulls found in an Egyptian cave prove that these animals were considered sacred," he wrote, "I see nothing implausible in the idea that our bear bones were similarly brought into the caves by human hands, and that they should be considered the remnants or proof of a pagan reverence."

Rosenmüller assumed that the bone gatherers had never seen the live animals themselves, and only later did scientists realize that early humans, cave bears, and other now-extinct animals must have lived at the same time. However, the conditions under which they coexisted remained unclear. Scholars in the early nineteenth century imagined that our ancestors, clad in fur and wielding nothing more than axes, would regularly battle bears ten to twelve feet tall with enormous humps of fat on their shoulders. The illustration at the beginning of this chapter shows just such a stirring (but, unfortunately, scientifically unfounded) scene.

Craniums of the cave bear (above) and the brown bear.

Surprisingly, researchers in the late nineteenth and early twentieth centuries had little respect for the mountains of bear bones they uncovered. The finds were so numerous that, as W. E. A. Zimmermann described in 1880, they were "carried off by the wagonload." Toward the end of the First World War, when the lack of access to guano from South America led to a scarcity of valuable phosphate dung in many places, earth from the caves—which, due to the bears' remains, was rich in phosphates—was used instead. During this time the "Dragon Caves" in Austria's Steiermark region were plundered. Only the skulls and leg bones found there were kept.

A great leap was made when the Swiss paleontologist Emil Bächler explored the "Dragon Hole" (such fossil-laden caverns seem to have been invariably linked with dragons in the popular imagination), a cave located more than seventy-three hundred feet above sea level and extending more than two hundred yards into a cliff in the Tamina valley. Bächler found well-preserved skulls and leg bones, but it was the so-called stone tables he discovered there that really caused a sensation. The researcher suggested that these tables had been built by early humans, who used them for making tools from stones and bones. He further described how the cave bear skulls and leg bones had been carefully sorted and stacked in special "stone boxes." Bächler assumed that these activities were carried out by members of a sacrificial cult and discussed how these trophies could have served as "hunting amulets." He was furthermore certain that the bears had lived between 120,000 and 130,000 years ago, during a period of the Ice Age in which warm phases occurred. Otherwise, he argued, glaciers would have prevented the Neanderthals from reaching the caves at all. Cave bears, according to Bächler, were therefore the most significant prey for early hunters. Konrad Hörmann, who investigated Peter's Cave in Bavaria, came to similar conclusions after he found fourteen cave bear skulls along with the bones of prehistoric humans. He promptly declared the cave to be a "sacred site of the ancient Paleolithic hordes." From then on, whenever caves were explored in Europe—whether in the Pyrenees, the Alps, the Caucasus, or the Urals—collections of bones and skulls came to light. As a result, the idea quickly spread that a "cave-bear hunter culture," in which bears played a prominent role in the life of humans, had existed during the Stone Age.

But was the evidence for this widespread culture really so convincing? One of the first scholars to take a completely different position was the Swiss scientist Felix Kolby. He claimed that the piles of bones had occurred by chance. Subsequent generations of animals had continued to inhabit the caves, Kolby argued, and moved about among the remains of their forebears. The criticism of renowned Finnish paleontologist Björn Kurtén was even harsher: Bächler's drawings showing the location of the bones in the cave were contradictory, he asserted, and since the "stone boxes" had been destroyed during the excavation they could not be used to prove the existence of the bear cult.

In a similar vein, the French archaeologist and paleontologist André Leroi-Gourhan considered the idea of a bear cult to be his field's "most popular playground for unfounded constructions." Leroi-Gourhan became skeptical after he discovered a "circle" of bones in a cave and published news of his findings. The dramatic theories his report inspired came as a surprise, as he suggested that the grouping of the bones was simply the result of the bears' behavior. In his view, as the bears moved about the strewn bones, they may have occasionally pushed some under the overhanging walls or between the blocks of stone. Over time, the bones thus collected in these out-of-the way niches and were saved from damage. Other researchers believed that the bear remains had accumulated over thousands of years. The number of animals living together in the caves thus would not have been as large as was sometimes assumed. In fact, as we now know, the majority of the cave bear skeletons came from animals that had sought out the caves to hibernate. It was not uncommon for ill or weak animals to die during this period of inactivity. If such deaths occurred even only occasionally at a particular location, a considerable number of bones could build up over the centuries— bones that researchers would later find in the sediment on the cave floors.

In more recent times, methods that scientists have developed to study the layers of sediment can help us determine when the cave bears lived. These studies suggest that although cave bears and humans lived during the same period, they sought out the caves at different times—in fact, no clear connection at all can be made between the bear bones and stone tools found in the caves. That humans ever even hunted cave bears can be proven only in rare and isolated cases. The fanciful suggestion of some early scientists—that limb bones in which small holes were visible had been

used as flutes—was also debunked: no trace could be found that the bones had been intentionally altered. All this was bad news for fans of the cave bear cult.

Bear painting from the cave at Chauvet, France.

However, we cannot forget the masterful image of a cave bear found in a deep limestone cavern in the Ardèche region in southern France. Painted some thirty-five thousand years ago, it is twice as old as the more famous images at Lascaux and those found at Altamira in northern Spain. However fascinating these well preserved images may be, they cannot really tell us what the relationship of humans and bears was like. Since the bear is depicted along with animals such as horses, bison, lions, and ancient oxen, the painting does not necessarily prove that bears occupied a special place in the world of the artist.

SO WHAT HAPPENED TO the cave bears? Did a meteorite or a comet exterminate them, along with the other great animals of the Ice Age? Or was a plague to blame? Did the bears degenerate due to inbreeding? One theory from the early twentieth century—now refuted—claimed that the bears essentially domesticated themselves by living in the caves and thus lacked the strength to survive the last Ice Age. Today some paleontologists believe that, as the summers grew shorter and shorter, the bears were forced to take on an enormous amount of fat to survive the long winters. This diet made them so heavy and slow that they could no longer hunt and lived only from plants. They managed to survive several cycles of the Ice Age, but when the climate grew even colder their ability to adapt was exhausted—they would lie down to hibernate and never wake up. This theory, however, is somewhat dubious, because many bears were in fact herbivores.

According to a recent genetic investigation by German evolutionary anthropologist Michael Hofreiter and his colleagues, the sudden disappearance of certain groups of cave bears in southern Germany in approximately 28,000 B.C. could be related to the arrival of modern humans in the Ach Valley by 35,000 B.C., as there is no evidence to suggest that any major climate change occurred around this time to influence the bears' fate. Hofreiter, however, is careful not to generalize his findings—for him, the truth for the disappearance of cave bears lies somewhere in the middle, between nonhuman and human causes. Therefore, as these findings suggest, the question of how exactly humans and cave bears interacted seems far from settled.

Der Waschbär
Procyon Lotor.
Le Raton Laveur

Kopf eines Jungen

Kopf des alten

Langrüssliger Bär. (Sehr alt)    Ursus longirostris    Le Jongleur.

# CHAPTER FOUR

# False Steps

Some animal illustrations produced hundreds of years ago resemble mythical beings more than the real-life creatures they are meant to represent. Depictions of brown bears, however, usually do not exhibit fanciful extremes, but rather more subtle errors: after all, their surface anatomy offers little opportunity for serious misunderstanding. They tend to appear more ungainly in old drawings than they do in reality. Sometimes, as in Edward Topsell's (?–1638) *History of Four-Footed Beasts,* the paws are disproportionately large, the ears are pointed like those of a cat, or the entire posture simply seems awkward. Their thick fur and the inch of fat beneath their skin can easily create the impression that bears are clumsy, but as we know from documentary films they are quite capable of quick, agile movements. When we look at the Albrecht Dürer map of the northern constellations in about 1515, both Ursa Minor, the Little Bear, and Ursa Major, the Great Bear, are shown with long tails. This mistake seems to be a way to accommodate the placement of the stars, since Dürer's drawings are otherwise recognized for their accuracy.

The theories of early nature writers about bears, in contrast, could be extremely creative. As French scientist Georges Buffon was compelled

Raccoon and sloth bear (1824), the latter characterized as a "bear with a long trunk, very old."

49

to complain, "Among at least the generally known animals, there is none about which the claims of researchers diverge so greatly as the bear."

The Roman writer Pliny the Elder (23–79 A.D.) informed us that bears mate in the winter. Then, he continued, the female retreats to her cave and, after thirty days, produces her young—in most cases, three. At birth the cubs are shapeless lumps of flesh barely larger than mice, and only their claws are developed. The mother then licks them into their proper shape. What—besides the obvious—is wrong with this account? Bears do not mate in winter, but rather from April to August. But Pliny could not have known that up to five months can pass after mating before the fertilized egg attaches to the wall of the uterus—a process that takes only three to four days in humans—and only then develops into a bear cub. Scientists call this phenomenon, regulated by hormonal processes, "delayed implantation." If the bear does not find enough food in the fall, hormonal processes cause the egg to be reabsorbed, thereby preventing the cubs' birth.

In 1785 Buffon, then director of the Jardin des Plantes in Paris, was of the opinion that bears carried their young for only thirty days and wrote that "since no one has disproved this idea and we have found no opportunity to verify it,

From Edward Topsell's book.

Early representation of a bear.

we can so little refute as accept it." However, Swedish naturalist and taxonomist Carolus Linnaeus (1707–1778) had already broken with the generally held opinion, believing that pregnancy in bears lasted 112 days. While his criticism of the ancients was justified, Linnaeus was nonetheless also wrong.

"Ursa major," by Albrecht Dürer.

Why embryos were never found in the bodies of female bears killed during the autumn remained a mystery well into the nineteenth century. Some writers, such as Reichenbach, simply chose to ignore this puzzling detail. Finally, in 1882 zoologist G. Herbst voiced the idea that the phenomenon of delayed implantation could occur in brown bears similar to the way it does in deer. Later biologists championed this theory, including G. W. D. Hamlett, who proposed it in 1935. However, the delayed implantation of brown bear embryos was not proven conclu-

Georges Buffon.

"Bearlike sloth" (1810).

"Syrian bear," by Heinrich Rudolf Schinz (1824), looks more like a dog than a slim bear.

sively until 1963, by biologists L. Dittrich and H. Kronberger. Since that time this process has been identified in more than one hundred animal species.

Pliny's belief that bear cubs are shaped after their birth by their mothers may have stemmed from the fact that the physical structure of cubs is not clearly visible at birth. They develop in the womb over a very brief time—that is, in about fifty-four days. A grizzly cub weighs only about nine ounces at birth, while a mother grizzly can easily weigh three hundred pounds—meaning she is some 529 times larger than her newborn. The ratio of human newborns to their mothers, in comparison, is about 1:25.

Pliny further claimed that the soles of bears' paws contain a great deal of fat, which the animals consume—in other words, that bears have the ability to eat from their own bodies. In 1703 Baron LaHontan reported that the Iroquois and Algonquin shared this belief: "Many people will not believe that the animals can spend three months [in hibernation] with only the juice from their paws as nourishment—but this fact is completely indisputable," he wrote. In actuality, the skin on bear paws regenerates during hibernation. Bears tend to audibly suck and chew on their paws during this time, probably in an attempt to soothe the resulting itching or discomfort.

In a book he published in 1734, Johann Täntzern considered the reproductive behavior of bears. One of his illustrations shows two sets of bears about to mate. While one of the couples appears in a genuine ursine mating position, the female bear of the second couple lies on her back on the floor with the male on top of her. Even Aristotle believed that bears had sex in the missionary position and wrote that they lie on the ground to mate. A twelfth-century bestiary also claimed that bears "do not love each other as other four-footed creatures do, but rather embrace and mate in the same manner as men and women." These misconceptions remained unrectified until the eighteenth century, when Buffon wrote that bears "come together in the autumn. The female is said to be more lustful than the male. Some claim that, in order to receive him, she lies on her back, embraces him, holds him fast, etc.; however, it is certain that they mate in same manner as other four-footed animals."

Between 1747 and 1751 Pehr Kalm, a student of Linnaeus, toured the American colonies. The reports of his travels include many descriptions of

the native animals and plants, including an account of a bear killing a cow by ripping a hole in its body and then blowing into this opening with all his might, causing the cow to swell up and die. This "observation" aroused a great deal of attention but was eventually exposed as a fabrication by American botanist John Bartram, who had hoodwinked the author.

Lorenz Oken of Germany, first a doctor and then a natural scientist, set out in the 1830s to "compare and report on everything ever observed about the life and behavior of animals and written in travelogues and newspapers since the earliest days." This monumental effort, according to Oken, consisted of unmasking "false citations," reading "a lot of useless nonsense," and comparing "a great number of bad and thoughtless illustrations." He considered bears to be not particularly aggressive because they attack people only if provoked. The bear, Oken reported, "leads an unhappy, quiet, and lonely life and only associates with the female during the mating season."

Slowly the bear was stripped of its role as man's cousin among the large mammals. In fact, Buffon's ideas about a common ancestry of apes and men had already shattered any residual belief in the kinship of humans and bears. His farsighted hypotheses anticipated Charles Darwin's research, which confirmed that primates are our closest animal relatives, thus making them the "aristocrats" among the animals.

In addition to the resemblance between the two species, however, people were equally fascinated by bears for other reasons, such as how they survived the winter. Unlike other animals, the bear does not gather and store food but rather enigmatically disappears for a time—rather like a tree that sheds its leaves and seems to die, only to flourish again in the spring. To many observers, this behavior must have seemed like a link between the realms of the living and the dead. For the Cree Indian tribe, archaeologist Marija Gimbutas pointed out, bear hibernation and waterfowl migration served as principal markers for the division of the year. Moreover, these animals provided "the basis for models of a seasonal symbiotic parallel between the social life of men and animals."

It should therefore not come as a surprise that humans developed astounding explanations to account for hibernation. Swiss naturalist Conrad Gessner (1516–1565), for example, seemed to rely in good faith on the unlikely report of a

Polar bear hibernating. (John George Wood, *Homes Without Hands,* 1866)

Swiss goatherd. One day in the late fall, the man claimed, as he left his hut with a cheese pot on his head, he saw a bear in the distance pick a plant and eat it. After the bear had left the area, the goatherd tasted the same plant himself, immediately lay down on the path, covered his head with the pot, and, despite the winter cold, slept until the onset of spring. Once a bear selects a suitable cave for his retreat, Gessner claimed, he backs into it as lightly as possible "so that the hunters do not come across his tracks." He wrote that, during the first two weeks of hibernation, bears sleep so soundly that they do not respond to anything, "no matter how great the uproar"; neither "blows, jabs, thumps nor injury" can wake them.

The Jakuts, in turn, believed that hibernating bears could still hear everything they said and therefore avoided speaking badly about them during this time. In the summer, they reasoned, the animals would be busy filling their stomachs and would not care much about what people had to say. In his *Animal Biography,* British naturalist William Bingley wrote: "As soon as the snow falls, the bear takes his repose, which lasts uninterrupted until the snow melts. This respite is not a true hibernation and even less a dormancy, but rather a mere lack of activity, a lying still, during which the bear neither takes in nourishment nor eliminates wastes." Not long afterward, philosophy professor Joseph Bonavita Blank stated: "The bear leads a lonely life, spends most of the winter without sustenance, and ceases to move, remaining senseless or sleeping as long as the ground is covered with snow." According to natural historian Anton B. Reichenbach, "In the wintertime they are drunken with sleep and do not leave their caves."

The fact that so little consensus existed about even the simplest facts is demonstrated by French physician Clément François Victor Gabriel Prunelle, who disputed that bears hibernate even in the coldest of periods and claimed never to have heard of anyone surprising an "insensate" bear. At the beginning of the winter, Prunelle explained, the bear becomes inactive and is no longer seen out in the open landscape around the Alps. If he is surprised in his lair he cannot run well because his paws have become tender "from sucking on them." Physician Adolph W. Otto shared Prunelle's view. He reported that he had kept a captive bear in a dark location in order to be able to observe him closely. When the bear fell asleep he could easily be awakened, and Otto described him as weak and despondent *(debilis et morosus)* rather than as sleepy. That his experiment had nothing to do with a bear's natural behavior does not seem to have troubled the good doctor. He could not know that captive bears simply don't hibernate.

While old folktales and legends don't explain why bears hibernate, they nevertheless express human preoccupation with this behavior. For example, an Estonian legend relates the story of a farmer and his wife who, on the Feast of St. Michael during the fall, when markets and celebrations were held, wanted to cook cabbage soup for supper. There was no more wood in the house, so the farmer went into the forest to fetch some. His search took him farther and farther from home until he lost his way. After walking for a long time he came across a bear's den and, too tired to go on, he went in and soon fell asleep. He awoke once during the night, but when he saw that it was still dark he turned over and went back to sleep. In the morning he awoke and found the way home. But his wife did not recognize him—the only familiar thing about him was his voice. The man was very hungry and asked if there was any leftover soup from what he assumed to have been the day before. His wife stared at him in amazement. "Didn't you cook the soup after all?" he asked. It turned out that the man had been gone all winter, and now spring had arrived and Annunciation Day, the twenty-fifth of March, had come and gone. Since then, the legend goes, the bears go into their dens every year on St. Michael's Day and hibernate.

What *do* bears do in winter? Do they sleep? Do they fall into a kind of paralysis? Do they rest, or are they overpowered by a weakness of some sort at the onset of winter? Today we know more: brown bears spend three to four months in the winter in a resting state, which can be understood as a less extreme form of genuine hibernation. In this way their winter habits differ from those of dormice or hedgehogs, who sleep uninterrupted for a long period each winter and thus truly hibernate. During this period of rest, the bear's pulse slows and its body temperature drops by about two and a half degrees. Winter is an arduous time for bears: foraging for food is extremely difficult, made all the more so by their relatively short legs, which are not suited for wading through snow. Entering a sleeplike state allows them to bypass the challenging winter. They prepare for this period of inactivity by accumulating fat during the months when food is plentiful.

We do know that bears are extremely creative in their choice of a sanctuary. Although they may seek out naturally occurring shelters, they are also capable of partially or completely creating a suitable den on their own. They can find shelter in forests or on mountains—even above the tree line, on extremely steep cliffs. Sometimes a den is used for decades by the same bear. Bears in Europe have been known to make use of at least ten possible types of winter dens, such as under the roots of a live tree; in a hollowed-out anthill; in a cave; under or between boulders; in a hole; in the branches or roots of fallen trees; in a hollow tree trunk; or under piles of fallen branches.

In 1888 the German magazine *The Huntsman* published a vivid account from Minsk written by Wilhelm, Prince Radziwill. He had observed a five-year-old male bear setting up its winter quarters in the branches of a white fir. "The trunk divided into three sections," Radziwill wrote, "and within the fork the animal had gathered together all the available twigs like a stork's nest in order to bed down in them. Once he got a bullet through the neck he slid at once down the trunk and came galloping [*sic*] to a halt on the ground." The bear most likely had been bothered by wolves in previous years and so planned to spend the coming winter well above the ground.

WE CONTINUE TO LEARN from bears. Recent research on hibernation has aroused great interest in the medical community. American biologist Seth W. Donahue has found that sleeping bears during the winter continue to build bone matter at a much higher rate than would normally be expected. His investigations, which are based on the analysis of blood samples, could lead to an effective treatment for osteoporosis. Henry J. Harlow, a zoology professor at the University of Wyoming, is concentrating on a different aspect of hibernation. A few years ago he discovered that black bears lose only about a quarter of their muscle strength during this five- to seven-month period, while humans would lose 90 percent during a comparable period of inactivity. Harlow suggested that certain processes occur during sleep to stimulate the bears' muscles, or that urea, produced as part of the breakdown of protein from the bear's fat reserves, has the effect of regenerating them.

# CHAPTER FIVE

# Exotic Discoveries

As Europeans explored new lands, they also discovered new bears. One of their most sensational finds, the panda, has perhaps since become the most beloved bear species of all. The animals live in southern China, in a formerly subtropical area that was pushed together into a mountainous region by tectonic activity and that today lies at the same latitude as northern Africa and California.

While pandas may seem to us to be the quintessential Chinese animal, their historical role in Chinese culture is difficult to ascertain. Descriptions of animals in early texts are sometimes so imprecise or contradictory that it is difficult to tell if the creatures in question are pandas at all. One possible candidate from a three-thousand-year-old songbook is an animal, called *pi,* that seems to resemble a tiger or a leopard. But in an early dictionary from the Qin dynasty (221–207 B.C.), the pi is said to be a white fox. The same source, however, also mentions a promising *mo,* a white "leopard" with a small head, short limbs, and (at least this part sounds like a leopard) black and white spots. Bai Juyi, a poet of the later Tang dynasty (618–907), had a different opinion: for him the mo "has the nose of an elephant, the eyes of a rhinoceros, the tail of an ox and the foot of a

Panda bears.

tiger"—a description that, in turn, sounds more like a tapir than a panda.

Later texts do not throw more light on the matter. A royal report from 685 A.D. mentions two "white bears" and seventy "white bearskins" sent from China to Japan. Although the report could have been referring to pandas, it also could have meant polar bears, which Chinese hunters could have captured or killed in the north of the continent. After all, Marco Polo is said to have seen polar bears during his Mongolian journey in the thirteenth century. It is also possible that the pelts stemmed from Himalayan bears, which admittedly do not have the characteristic black-and-white patterning of pandas, but which do have large cream-colored spots on their chests. Further complicating matters is the existence of another possible candidate—a relative of the brown bear with silvery fur—that lives in a region adjoining the area in which pandas are found.

In the Chinese *Materia Medica,* a comprehensive collection of medical knowledge from 1597, the panda, or *bei-shung,* is not mentioned at all. This omission is particularly surprising because the Chinese ascribed healing powers to almost every part of every animal imaginable. One explanation for this gap is that the bodies of pandas were not used for medical purposes because the animals possessed special religious significance. However, the fact that pandas play no role whatsoever in Chinese folklore argues against this theory. But regardless of the meaning early inhabitants of China may have ascribed to the panda, a

2005 discovery proves beyond a doubt that they had contact with these bears. In a four-thousand-year-old grave in the central region of the country, archaeologists discovered both a human skeleton and panda remains. At first the scientists mistakenly believed that the jawbone they found was that of a pig, but genetic analysis proved that it in fact came from a panda.

Western science, in turn, became aware of pandas just less than 150 years ago—on March 11, 1869, to be precise. On that day, a Chinese landowner named Li invited French missionary and naturalist Father Armand David, who was working with the Lazarists in Beijing, to tea. At Li's house, David saw a panda pelt. In his excitement he convinced a few hunters to show him such a bear. Two weeks later they brought him a specimen—dead, unfortunately. David described the bear as "a new species of *Ursus,* which is very remarkable not only for its color, but also because of that fact that it has fur on the underside of its paws, and for other characteristics." Shortly thereafter, David wrote to zoologist Sir Henry Milne-Edwards, who was in Paris. Realizing that it would take several months for the specimens to reach him, he asked Milne-Edwards to publish the description of his discovery, *Ursus menanoleuca,* as soon as possible. David wrote that he had never encountered the animal in a European museum and believed it to be new to science, adding, "It is the most beautiful creature I know of."

In 1870 David brought the bear to Paris, and the next year Milne-Edwards sent the following

Father Armand David.

report to the Museum of Natural History: "This bear, which hunters call *Paé-shioung* (white bear), is very much rarer than the black Tibetan bear that inhabits the same forests. It is found at much higher altitudes and appears to have a vegetable diet. Nevertheless, it does not refuse flesh when the occasion presents itself; and I even believe that this is its principal means of nourishment in winter, as it does not spend this season sleeping." Although the great panda was by now becoming known among zoologists, the public's only exposure to this rare bear species was a single stuffed specimen. The name "harlequin bear" favored by some scientists failed to catch on. No one knows where the name "panda" came from, but it may derive from *niyalaya-ponga,* or "bamboo eater."

The great panda quickly became one of the world's most coveted trophies, and many hunters made their way to central Sichuan. Such a trip was not without its dangers: panda hunter Lieutenant J. W. Brooke, for example, was murdered by the inhospitable Lolos in 1910. It was also no mean feat to spot a panda in the wild in the first place. Zoologist Hugo Weigold, who took part in an expedition during the First World War in western China and eastern Tibet, was lucky enough to spot fresh bear tracks and set his dogs on the trail. But all he ever saw were branches swinging wildly in the wake of a creature he never glimpsed. He later bought a panda from the local inhabitants, which unfortunately soon died because of a lack of appropriate food.

In 1928, the sons of U.S. president Theodore

"Teddy" Roosevelt, Theodore and Kermit, set off with the promise that they would not return before successfully bagging a panda. Despite their extensive financial resources and intensive preparation, they were soon forced to concede that the wild mountain regions of Sichuan were nearly inaccessible and frequented by dangerous bandits. Further complicating matters, Kermit Roosevelt reported, was the problem that information provided by natives proved to be wholly unreliable. The brothers therefore decided to believe only what they could see with their own eyes: the bears' excrement, which the animals' diet of bamboo and plant stalks made easy to identify. Tracks in the snow offered further clues to the pandas' whereabouts. The dogs that they had organized locally, however, were of little help, as they turned out to be unsuitable for hunting.

Despite all the warnings, the Roosevelt brothers also contacted the notorious Lolos: "On the morning of the 13th April we came upon giant panda tracks in the snow near Yelhi, south of Tchienlu in the Hsifan Mountains," Kermit wrote. "The animal had evidently passed a goodish while before the snow ceased falling, but some sign that one of the Lolos found proved to be recent enough to thoroughly arouse all four natives." After tracking the animal for more than two hours, Kermit continued, he heard a "clicking chirp." "One of the Lolo hunters darted forward. He had not gone forty yards before he turned back to eagerly motion us to hurry. As I gained his side he pointed to a giant spruce thirty yards away. The bole was hollowed, and from it emerged the head and forequarters of a bei-shung. He looked sleepily from side to side and he sauntered forth and walked slowly away into the bamboos. As soon as Ted came up we fired simultaneously at the outline of the disappearing panda. Both shots took effect. He was a splendid old male, the first that the Lolos had any record of as being killed in this Yehli region."

News of the "success" of the two hunters circled the globe, and their trophy was later exhibited in Chicago's Museum of Natural History. The world today might be less inclined to celebrate their deed: they thought nothing of killing the rare bear, although their report depicts the panda as a gentle creature that did not even utter a sound as it was shot. They also sparked a bout of panda-hunting fever in the years that followed, as every self-respecting American museum wanted to acquire such a specimen. As late as 1935, the journal *Natural History* published an extensive report on a panda hunt near the border of China and Tibet, although the same publication had complained just a few years earlier that mammals hunted for their pelts would die out. Interest shifted shortly thereafter to capturing the animals rather than killing them, and in 1937 the first panda living in captivity could be seen at the Chicago Zoo.

For decades, the giant panda was a widely recognized symbol of all endangered species. But recent research suggests that the number of these animals living in the wild has apparently been underestimated: British and Chinese biologists, working with Michael Bruford of the University of Wales in Cardiff, recently discovered that the panda population is considerably larger than previously believed. Since the animals' timidity and wariness make it virtually impossible to simply locate and count them, the scientists used DNA analysis to investigate the panda excrement found within a ten-square-mile wildlife preserve. They systematically collected heaps of panda dung and analyzed the genetic material, eventually determining that between sixty-six and seventy-two of the black and white bears live in the Wanglang Reservation, the world's oldest panda preserve. Before Bruford's study, only twenty-seven animals were known to inhabit the area.

Bruford believes that similar numbers of "hidden" pandas exist at other wildlife parks—enough animals to make up a total population of 2,500 to 3,000. Previously, only 1,590 pandas were thought to populate the mountains of central and southern China, the animal's present-day habitat. But Bruford sees no cause for jubilation, because this population is still small nevertheless, and so the species will continue to need the protection of the Chinese government.

WERE THERE EVER BEARS in Africa? Dutch geographer Olfert Dapper claimed to have seen them there in the seventeenth century, along with wild pigs. Were the *karrai,* animals with large snouts exterminated by the natives of Abyssinia, in fact bears, or were they hyenas or wild dogs? Was the "black bear" that German zoologist Christian Gottfried claimed to have seen in Abyssinia at the beginning of the nineteenth century—and one that he unsuccessfully attempted to kill—really a bear at all? Pliny's opinion, at least, is clear: *Africa ursos non gigni constat,* there are no bears in Africa.

However, many sources, including early ones, contradict Pliny's sweeping statement. During the rule of the consuls Messala and Piso, a Roman official named Domitius Ahenobarbus is said to have brought a hundred bears to the Roman circus from Numidia, a region that covered large areas of today's Algeria and Tunisia. Charlemagne supposedly received his own Numidian bear as a gift from an African emir in 801. Could these accounts simply be fantasy? Since the Berbers have no word for bear, despite designating all other mammals, birds, and even the tiniest of creatures with unique names, Baron Henri Aucapitaine assumed in 1860 that bears did not exist in the region—and never had. Furthermore, bears do not appear in the Sahara cliff drawings, although these remarkable artworks depict elephants and rhinoceroses, animals that had long vanished from the area by the time the drawings were made. According to some researchers, however, the drawings were the work of travelers who had seen the animals they depicted much farther south.

Aucapitaine's claim is all the more surprising because he surely knew that Henry Milne-Edwards—the same zoologist who would later report on Armand David's panda specimen—had already found the remnants of a bear skull in Algeria, between Oran and Mers-el-Kabir, in 1835. A year earlier, two bears were reputedly captured in Morocco and investigated by a man named Crowther, who drew a clear distinction between his discoveries and Syrian bears and reported that they fed on roots, acorns, and fruit. The females, according to Crowther, were smaller and fatter than American black bears, and their faces were shorter and broader. Working from these reports, Swiss physician and zoologist Heinrich Rudolf Schinz introduced the name *Ursus crowtheri* into the scientific literature in 1842, although the same animals were also referred to, less exaltedly, as "Berber bears."

When Jules René Bourguignat searched various caves in northwest Africa in the 1860s, he uncovered the bones of an animal that he first dubbed simply "new bear," or *Ursus nouveau*. His subsequent discovery of a burial lamp typical of the Roman period nearby convinced him that bears existed in Algeria around the time of Christ's birth. These animals, Bourguignat reasoned, were small and compact, with short legs and relatively large heads. The absence of prominent incisors suggests that these animals primarily ate fruit . Bourguignat named the animal *Ursus faidherbianus,* after Louis Léon César Faidherbe, the former French governor of Senegal. Faidherbe established the country's borders, which have remained the same to this day.

Bourguignat, whose tendency to classify animals with abandon made him a controversial figure, admitted that "in his book about his travels to the Barbary Coast in 1785–86, Abbé Poiret said that bears cannot stand the hot African climate and only feel at home in ice and snow." The zoologist countered, however, that a preference for such a habitat did not rule out the presence of bears in the Maghreb, since "the Atlas rise up to great heights from the kingdom of Algeria to Morocco, so that several mountains are almost always capped with snow." The bears, Bourguignat continued, "eat a great deal of meat and sometimes descend into the valleys." He further related that during his stay in La Mazoule, near Ali-Bey, "an Arab brought the skin of a bear he had killed" and claimed that "this same Arab also showed me an injury to his leg that he had received when the bear he later killed had thrown rocks at him."

The number of those believing that there had never been bears in Africa continued to dwindle. However, the bears that once populated the continent apparently disappeared for good in the middle of the nineteenth century. At the end of the 1990s a French scientist and his Algerian colleague used the carbon-dating method to show that the bones of a small bear found in the Djurdjura cave date from 420 to 600 A.D.

No one knows whether bears were also native to Egypt. The bears presented to various pharaohs as tribute could have been brought from countries farther to the east. In biblical times, brown bears were common in Palestine, and there is evidence that they also lived in the mountainous regions of the Sinai Peninsula, which in earlier times were covered with forests. In 1738 a man named Richard Pockocke wrote that the *dubber* (the Arabic word for *bear* that is now transcribed as *dubb*) was seen only rarely in Egypt. The word *dubber* was long used not only for bears, but also for hyenas, so it is impossible to know for sure whether ancient texts containing the term actually refer to bears or—the more likely case—to the latter. However, since Pockocke added the ending *hahena* to indicate a hyena, his comment about Egypt seems to pertain to actual bears. According to his account, the animals there were similar to Syrian bears but somewhat slimmer and with lighter-colored fur. He also described the *dubber* as having a short tail, providing further evidence that the creature he described could not have been a hyena. After Pockocke, no traveler to Egypt reported seeing bears there.

If what happened to the bears is a mystery, so too is how they got to North Africa in the first place. According to French biogeographer Nicolas Manlius, they most likely came to northern Egypt and Libya over the Suez isthmus. The oak and cedar forests that existed there until about 10,000 B.C. would have provided a good environment for bears. They may also have reached Africa via any of several straits: between the Iberian Peninsula and present-day Morocco, between Sicily and Tunisia, or even between the Arabian Peninsula and Ethiopia—even though easily passable land bridges probably never existed there. Bears are, after all, good swimmers: grizzly bears have been observed swimming to islands up to eight miles from the mainland. The bears' disappearance from North Africa, in turn, was likely the result of the destruction of the initially welcoming environment. Only two thousand years ago, forests could be found throughout the region, but they fell victim to a need for lumber and grazing land for sheep and goats.

BEARS ARE USUALLY considered native to forested regions, whether cold, temperate, or warm, but not to the steppe or the desert. So it is no surprise that they do not play a central role in the culture of the Arabian Peninsula. Still, bears were known there as visitors and members of the circle of wild animals, and were probably caught in the forests of nearby Lebanon or the mountains of Iraq. Although most Eurasian people considered bear meat a delicacy, in Arabia strict taboos discouraged its consumption. Bear meat was also considered difficult to digest and fattening as well. However, common wisdom did hold that bear fat, applied topically, could help cure a number of illnesses or prevent hair loss.

The Arabian fable of the bears and the monkeys may offer a fanciful explanation for the lack of bears in the region. The bears, according to the story, had driven their rivals from their fruit tree–filled kingdom, killing many monkeys as a result. When the bears encountered the monkey Maimon, he pretended that his king had mistreated him because he advised against attacking the monkeys' powerful enemy. Maimon then convinced the bears that he would guide them to a place where the monkeys were gathering a mighty army. But instead the clever monkey led the bears into the desert, where they all died from the heat.

# CHAPTER SIX

# The Bear's Personality

As we have seen, it has been the bear's fate to serve as a yardstick for humans. Giovanni Battista della Porta (1535–1615), an Italian naturalist and one of the first scientists in the modern sense, classified various human types according to the animals they supposedly resembled. For him, the bear embodied a whole series of negative characteristics: both the "coarse, uncultivated" person, with his large head and protruding mouth, and the "wrathful" person, with his deeply hollowed nostrils and thick beard, possess bearlike traits in his scheme. The "worst possible human character of all" was, for della Porta, the thoroughly bestial, "godforsaken idiot." This personality is revealed by dark eyes, a large belly, and a mouth that is "so long and wide . . . that the face seems split in two." Such an individual resembles the "ferocious bear," whom della Porta condemned as stupid, scheming, dangerous, treacherous, and, as if this were not enough, "wilder than all other animals," thus uniting lack of intelligence with cruelty and coarseness in one unlikable package.

Edward Topsell, who was most interested in the bear's physical characteristics, also made a few comments about the animal's psychology. He stated that "a Beare is of a most venerous and

Brown bear and corresponding images of a human with bear traits (eighteenth century).

lustful disposition." Topsell characterized bears of the "Helvetian alpine region" to be "full of courage," but added the qualification that "they will not willingly fight with a man." However, Topsell didn't seem to have considered the ways in which comparisons with bears might shed light on the mental makeup of humans.

ANIMAL PSYCHOLOGY, in turn, already existed as a marginalized branch of the sciences by the middle of the eighteenth century, but it didn't reach its height in the popular press until the nineteenth century. The discipline employed categorizations that were easy to grasp and thus appealed to many people. Its practitioners granted animals a measure of consciousness, along with emotions and the basis of an ego, and were interested above all in the question of whether or not specific behaviors were inborn or learned, and if animals were capable of remembering. This perspective was in sharp contrast to the ideas of René Descartes, who believed that animals were soulless automatons.

Jacques Henri Bernardin de Saint-Pierre (1737–1814) championed the view—which in his day enjoyed serious scientific consideration—that lions, through loving human care, could be transformed into gentle, vegetarian creatures. Saint-Pierre went so far as to claim that every animal is tame by nature and becomes wild only as a result of negative experiences. He even argued for a new kind of zoo in which kindly treatment and friendship between humans and animals would render the cruelties of confinement unnecessary.

Swiss science author Peter Scheitlin (1779–1848), one of the forerunners of the animal-rights movement, viewed the bear, which he considered to be a "most remarkable animal," as a thoroughly intelligent and good-natured creature, which when tamed can precisely distinguish among the three types of humans it encounters: its master (owner), benefactor (keeper), and superior (trainer). According to Scheitlin, bears know that they must make long detours through the forests and mountains to evade pursuers, and they have such a good sense of direction that they always find their way home. "'Angry as a mother bear robbed of her young' is a common saying," he reported. "Their love is uncommonly intense." Elsewhere in his book, Scheitlin claimed that the bear's skill in hunting, its dietary preferences, and its footprint all betray an affinity to human beings. Waxing truly euphoric, he even rhapsodized that a bear, out of principle, will touch nothing that is dead and likewise harms

A peaceful encounter in the forest.

no innocent beings. "He is known to have approached young girls hunting for strawberries and stolen the fruit right from their baskets, and then went on his way—we can almost dare to say —laughing," he wrote. "At the very least, he was surely laughing in his heart."

While Scheitlin's bear is almost insufferably lovable, a newcomer to the scientific world—the grizzly—was making a far different impression. "The African Lion, or the Tiger of Bengal, are not more terrible or fierce. He is the enemy of man, and literally thirsts for human blood. So far from shunning, he seldom fails to attack; and even to hunt him," wrote H. M. Brackenridge in 1814. Of course, this nightmarish characterization posed a serious obstacle to any deeper study of the bear's true characteristics.

Much later, in the 1880s, Theodore Roosevelt went west and devoted considerable attention to the grizzly, which he dubbed "Old Ephraim" during various hunting trips. He came to consider the bear "the King of game beasts of temperate North America" and "the mighty lord of the wilderness . . . the most dangerous to the hunter." He took the animal's name as a reference to its character and not to its grizzled gray fur—"in the same sense as horrible, exactly as we speak of a 'grisly spectre,'—and not *grizzly;* but perhaps the latter way of spelling it is too well established to be now changed." Despite this sweeping generalization, Roosevelt also claimed that bears differ in temperament just as people do: "There are savage and cowardly bears, just as there are big and little ones; and sometimes these variations are very marked among bears of the same districts."

An avid hunter, he believed that the animals had developed an awareness of the violent intentions of the humans they encountered. "Nowadays these great bears are undoubtedly much better aware of the death-dealing power of men," he reasoned, "and, as a consequence, are much less fierce than was the case with their forefathers, who so unhesitatingly attacked the early Western travellers and explorers." But Roosevelt went far beyond asserting that individual bears can learn—he attributed to the animals a remarkable ability to hand down knowledge to their descendants. "Constant contact with rifle-carrying hunters, for a period extending over many generations of bear-life, has taught the grizzly by bitter experience that man is his undoubted overlord," he wrote, "and this knowledge has become an hereditary characteristic." But lest the relative cowardliness of the modern grizzly throw doubt on his own hunting heroics, Roosevelt added that a wounded or cornered animal "will attack his foes with a headlong, reckless fury that renders him one of the most dangerous of the wild beasts."

Alongside the "proud lion," the "impish sparrow," and the "industrious ant," Alfred Brehm (1829–1884), the celebrated German "father of the animals," also studied the behavior and character of the bear. This son of a minister and ornithologist, who grew up among thousands of stuffed birds and who actually wanted to be an architect, accompanied Baron John von Müller on a five-year African expedition. Brehm and von Müller traveled through Egypt and the Sudan, where they barely escaped starvation, fought wild animals, and encountered angry natives who mistook them for slave traders. After the ex-

Alfred Brehm in Hamburg's Zoological Garden.

pedition, Brehm lived in Jena, where his student quarters resembled a zoo: with him resided a monkey, parrots, and a mongoose. His entirely negative portrayal of the bear is all the more astounding given his reputation as an unqualified animal lover who fought to save many species of wild animals and birds.

Brehm condemned the bear as thoroughly "unlikable" and a "dull-witted and spiritless fellow." One of his early articles further libeled the bear as "the notorious overlord of the animal kingdom" and an "unintentionally laughable fellow" who "does not deserve the respect he enjoys." He concluded that "the damage caused by bears is roughly balanced out by their usefulness to us" and lists a "first-class pelt" and "meat, bones and intestines" as examples of the bear's gifts to mankind.

In contrast to Brehm, Swiss hunter and naturalist Friedrich von Tschudi (1820–1886) emphasized the bear's "comfortable humor" as well as its jocular, amiable nature. For Tschudi, the bear had "a direct, open character free of cunning and deceit." The bear is far from harmless, however: "What the fox obtains with his wits and the eagle with his swiftness, the bear pursues with undisguised force." This view was echoed by A. Krementz, who based his assessment on his own observations while hunting in Russia rather than on the reports of unreliable witnesses. "He has an enormous love of comfort," Krementz wrote, "and his attacks betray a certain candor, directness, and courtliness that has nothing in common with the cowardly murderousness of the wolf or the deceptive cunning of the lynx."

Friedrich von Tschudi.

If we turn back to Brehm, we seem to be reading about an entirely different animal. "Any cat or dog is more able-witted," he insisted. "His seeming good nature is due from his lack of hunting skill, and the jovial impression he makes is imparted primarily by his form. The cat is courageous and the dog clever; the bear is stupid, coarse and rude." At another point he wrote, "The bear's every act betrays a weak, low and uneducable spirit." He even criticized the bear for avoiding "close association with civilized man" and claimed that "the wolf most definitely occupies a higher position and must be acknowledged as the nobler animal. . . . We can at best compare the bear to the swine: like him, the bear finds anything that is enjoyable to be acceptable."

Brehm further asserted that bears can never be trusted. He considered the animals worthy at best of a place behind bars at the zoo or at the side of a traveling animal trainer.

Zoology professor Gustav Jäger was of the opinion that the bear presented a "kaleidoscopic" figure like few other animals—and he did not intend this characterization as a compliment. Like the lion and the tiger, the bear can bring down the largest of mammals, yet it poaches the fields "like any mere ruminating beast." It steals from orchards and vineyards "like a monkey," eats berries from the stem "like a blackbird," climbs after pinecones "like a squirrel," plunders beehives and anthills "like a woodpecker," digs for maggots and worms "like a pig," and, finally, fishes and crabs "like an otter." In Jäger's view, the bear's personality is as complex as its tastes in food. "On the one hand," he wrote, "the bear is a fearsome combatant—equipped, as our forefathers claimed, with the strength of twelve men—who coolly challenges men and often overpowers them." "On the other, though," he continued, the bear is "a cowardly fellow, who lets himself be driven from the fields by a girl or an old woman wielding a basin or a hoe, and who plays the fool for children at the fair; who is led around, dancing like a monkey, or sits in the cage of a zoo saying 'pretty please' like a poodle." In his indignation, Jäger completely overlooked the fact that it was humans who forced the bear into the position of laughingstock.

Ludwig Heck, a director of the Berlin Zoo who

lost the tips of the first two fingers on his left hand to a bear, understood why the public loved bears "as much as they did monkeys," yet did not share this fascination himself. According to Heck, the bear "serves as a caricature of mankind, as our own distorted reflection." Such moments of recognition occur, Heck claimed, "when he stands on his hind legs and toddles around like a portly old man in his underwear, when he sits on his backside and 'lays his hands in his lap,' or when he, with astounding dexterity, gestures with his front paws, which resemble human hands in thick gloves and which are capable of the same rotational movement that makes our own hands the ready tools of our minds." As supposed proof of the bear's inferior character, Heck cited the so-called Drama in the Polar Bear Cage incident, in which a polar bear in the Cologne zoo had killed "his" female. The event was trumpeted in the newspapers of the day as a "wife murder." The fact that male bears in the wild live with females for only short periods, and thus—unlike lions and tigers, for example—are not "natural born husbands," was of course not as widely reported.

Karl Oberländer, who traveled through northern Russia just after the turn of the twentieth century, argued vehemently against naturalists who "assumed that the bear's shape indicated coarseness and clumsiness." It is wrong, Oberländer argued, "to judge a wild species across the board based on single individuals and isolated observations" and to attribute stupidity, cowardice, laziness, gentleness, or directness to bears in particular, since members of this species above all demonstrate "a rare diversity of character."

The tendency to describe the bear in terms of other animals reached its peak in 1911 when the naturalist Theodor Zell wrote, "When he stands upright, the bear resembles a gigantic man, while on all fours he looks more like an enormous pig. . . . Like lions, tigers, jaguars, and the like he has little endurance for running, and like these cats he has two weapons: his bite and his claws." But Zell warned against hastily concluding that bears and cats share a close kinship. The bear lacks the "flexibility of the cat" but possesses greater strength. According to Zell, bears actually have much more in common with dogs—both species have nonretractable claws and rely on their noses above all other sense organs. Zell even labeled the bear an "olfactory animal," a trait evidenced by its highly developed snout, and claimed that the animal's sense of sight is correspondingly underdeveloped. "When we compare the flashing, clear, large eye of the lion with a bear's uncertain little pig's eye, we immediately realize that these predators must belong to completely distinct classes, based on the difference in their fundamental senses." For Zell, the polar bear's long neck and narrow head, in turn, reveal the animal to be "an enormous winter weasel."

American biologist Enos A. Mills (1870–1922) championed the view that the grizzlies were smarter than horses, dogs, and even coyotes because they can process their experiences in particularly intelligent ways. Unlike his many German colleagues, who could observe bears only on the grounds of the zoological garden, Mills could relate a number of impressive cases of grizzlies in the wild who eluded hunters and trappers for years or even decades. One such bear was the famous "Old Mose," an "outlaw grizzly" whose habit of killing horses and cows earned him a bounty of a thousand dollars on his head. Despite the avid pursuit such a fortune inspired, this remarkable animal managed to survive thirty-five years in a territory just seventy-five miles across. This extraordinary intelligence seemed to have filled Mills with respect. "The grizzly is so dignified and so strangely human-like that I have felt degraded every time I have seen him pursued with dogs," he wrote. "A few times I have outwitted him; more often he has outwitted me. We have occasionally met unexpectedly; sometimes each stared without alarm, and at other times each fled in an opposite direction. Sometimes the grizzly is guided by instinct, but more often his actions are triumphantly directed by reason."

Is there a reliable way to describe the character of bears beyond the fact that they are often unpredictable? While the foregoing catalogue of contradictions may not reveal much about bears themselves, it surely demonstrates the extent to which humans have been moved to project human characteristics—both positive and negative—onto them. We have seen bears as good-natured, lazy, and even stupid, and at other times

Kopf 1
♂, etwa 4jährig, Zoo Berlin-W.;
aus Nord-Peru eingeführt

Kopf 2
♂, etwa 8jährig, Tierpark
Berlin-Friedrichsfelde;
aus Peru eingeführt

Kopf 3
♂, etwa 2jährig, Zoo Dresden;
aus Nord-Peru eingeführt

Kopf 4
♀, 11jährig, Zoo Basel;
im Zoo B. Aires geb.,
Eltern aus Ecuador

Kopf 5
♂, ³/₄jährig, Zoo Berlin-W.;
im Zoo Berlin geboren 1960

Kopf 6
♀, etwa 8—12jährig
Zoo Berlin-W.;
Herkunft unbekannt

Kopf 7
♀, 5jährig, Zoo Basel;
im Zoo B. Aires geboren,
Eltern aus Ecuador?

Kopf 8
♂, etwa 2jährig, Zoo Dresden;
aus Nord-Peru eingeführt

Kopf 9
♀, 11jährig, Zoo Basel;
im Zoo B. Aires geb.,
Eltern aus Ecuador

Kopf 10
♀, etwa 8—12jährig, Tierpark
Berlin-Friedrichsfelde;
Herkunft unbekannt

Abb. 7. Übersicht über die Verschiedenartigkeit der Gesichtszeichnung bei Brillenbären
(schematisiert dargestellt). — Zeichnung: Dr. S. RAETHEL (1958) und Dr. Dr. H. H. ROTH (1960)

as wrathful, deceitful, and unpredictable. The same animals that are labeled as cautious and suspicious are also painted as sly and cunning, wise and fearless, clever, brilliant, powerful, beautiful, and even majestic. We may assume that our ability to bestow such labels is a sign of our superiority over animals. Whether this is true or not, however, one thing at least seems to be clear: no matter how much it may look like one, a bear is not a man in fur.

Unlike other bear species, individual spectacled bears can be identified by the patterns on their faces.

Druck v. J. Braunsdorf, Dresden.

1. 2. 3. Gemeiner brauner Landbär. 4. Nordamerikanischer schwarzer Bär. Baribal. 5. Malayischer oder R
kragenbär. 6. Spielende Bären. 7. Dachs. 8. Eisbär eine Robbe od. Seehund verzehrend. 9. Waschbär od. Schu

# CHAPTER SEVEN

# Sounds, Senses, Signals

Aristotle distinguished between animals that make vocal noises and those that do not, while those animals gifted with voices may or may not be able to express articulated sounds. Without a doubt, the bear counts as an animal gifted with a voice. But what sounds, besides roaring, belong to the bear's repertoire? And to what extent are we capable of understanding its vocalizations?

"When he is angry, he gnashes his teeth, snorts and roars violently. At other times his voice is a low hum," wrote naturalist and Church of England clergyman William Bingley in 1805. Hunter Georg Franz Dietrich aus dem Winckell expressed a similar opinion in 1822: "One generally hears bears emit a roaring sound only when they are angry, but at times it can also indicate a certain well-being. In the first case, the roar is usually accompanied by an audible gnashing of the teeth." And, in an uncharacteristically terse comment in an otherwise detailed description from 1847, Anton Benedikt Reichenbach wrote that the bear's "face, hearing, and sense of touch are all refined. His voice is a low, hollow roar."

These passages illustrate the difficulty in de-

Various kinds of bears (1868).

scribing the sounds made by bears. Can the voices of animals be captured in words at all? In 1886, zoologist Philipp Leopold Martin tried to record animal sounds using musical notation. However, he could not assume that travelers had the necessary training to describe what they heard correctly. For this reason, Martin decided that a more practical solution was to compare animal sounds with known voices and to record additional criteria such as the animal's age and sex, its mood, and the point of time the observation was made (such as "during the mating period"). In 1891, his colleague Carl Grevé spoke out for a greater appreciation of "the modulated humming songs of the bear licking its paws." "So little attention is paid to the various tones emitted by the mammals, just because they are raw and, by our standards, not beautiful," Grevé complained, "while the 'song' of birds has lured many a researcher to depict their *sounds* with notes."

An attempt to develop a formal theory of animal sounds did not occur until the 1930s, at which time Karl Max Schneider, the director of the Leipzig Zoo, wrote, "It seems to me that vocal utterance—to the extent its form is not predetermined by instinct, such as some bird songs or other sound systems serving a social function (the roaring of lion or hyenas, the whinnying of horses, etc.)—is one of the most interpretable forms of animal expression. Most such sounds are even produced by organs similar to those of man. In the many graduations of their inflection, in their flexibility and correlation to changing circumstances, they are among, in my opinion, the most vital characteristics of the animal capable of producing them."

The object of his study was the baby polar bear Nanok, born in December 1931. Among Nanok's first vocal utterances recorded by Schneider were crying "in various intonations" as well as a humming or singing during nursing that he had already heard from brown bear cubs. The crying, he further specified, was like a drawn-out bleating that sounded like *ah* underlaid with *r,* and was sometimes mixed with squeaks. He also identified a "moaning," similar to the sound of a frog, which he felt expressed mild dissatisfaction. According to Schneider, this noise could—according to the situation—sink or rise "and thus display a certain melodic movement." Sometimes the "moaning" could also develop into a "squealing" like that made by young pigs. His young charge also produced hunting sounds, and Schneider determined that such "suckling, voiced 'm' sounds coming rhythmically every one to one and a half seconds" were "beautiful music for the zookeeper, for then he knows that the newborns are nursing."

At the age of ten and a half weeks, Nanok could produce "speech-like sounds that unmistakably expressed discontentment." Four weeks later, these sounds had evolved into a kind of roaring, and after a few more months Nanok's voice exhibited an even greater change: for the first time, he conveyed his irritation with "a sinking sigh that terminated in a long, low roar . . . he had been upset during the day and ran constantly back and forth, wouldn't eat, and was afraid to go into the sleep cage because a new companion—a young brown bear—was present."

When Nanok appeared to want something badly, he would make his wishes clear with "whines, grunts, or sighs." These discordant grunting calls would begin at a high pitch and then sink in waves, as if the animal were begging. This performance was often followed by a high but faint whine. In adult animals, Schneider reported, this sound could mount to a "breathy sigh of *ao* that resembled a foghorn."

If Schneider reprimanded his charge during these bouts of begging, Nanok would get louder and louder until, his mouth wide open, he emitted scratchy cries of *a(r)* that remained at the same pitch but grew more intense, as though he were insisting. These cries could turn into a bleating that lasted for hours, which in turn darkened a few months later in the direction of an *o* sound, taking on a hollow quality. Likewise, the whining, which Schneider's colleagues also referred to as "howling," could become a defiant "execration."

In addition to these "primary types of calls," Schneider documented two other methods of vocal communication: Nanok would snort and he would "pop" his lips. These sounds, neither of which was produced directly in the larynx, often alternated. If Schneider moved his hand in Nanok's direction, the bear would immediately begin to snort loudly, push out his upper lip like a trunk, and let out a deep roar. According to Schneider, "This snorting is produced as an investigation through scent intensifies. When bears encounter a new object, they place their noses on it like a vacuum cleaner, breath in deeply, and then exhale sharply and audibly." Among adult bears, this blowing through the nose could even become a "rumbling."

Polar bears snort loudly when something surprises them. This snorting can seem threatening and resemble "an agitated reproach or other form of insult," as Schneider explained. Nanok was four months old when Schneider first heard him produce "lip-popping" sounds "as an accompaniment to almost every stimulus. . . . It occurs when the breath is blown forcefully into the cheeks rather than the nose, whereby the mouth half-opens with a light pop as if from a small explosion. This seems to be a behavior unique to the large bears." He further recorded how the bears converse in this way during mating season. The female in particular has a tendency to pop her lips, a sound that to Schneider suggested "the effusion of unsatisfied longing." However fascinating we may find this catalogue of "call forms," we must remember that we can understand the true feel-

ings and emotions of bears only approximately, if at all.

IF BEARS ARE SUCH VOCAL artists, can they imitate the sounds of their prey? Attracting elks by imitating their deep mating calls and then attacking them is a trick "of which one can hardly hold the moody, ungainly fellow capable," the hunter Krementz wrote, although "experienced rangers have solemnly sworn this many times." He also recorded having such an experience himself during an elk hunt: "No further than 60 to 70 steps away from the deer hidden in the bushes, I suddenly heard a peculiar sound faintly resembling an elk's mating call from the thick brush to my left. However, the pitch and lack of clarity of this sound immediately awakened my suspicions while, as it repeated several times, inspiring both uneasiness and hope in the deer. Then—as the sound of breaking wood made clear—the figure from which the sounds seemed to emanate rushed forward in the deer's direction, emerged suddenly with a great deal of noise, and let out a mighty roar."

Today's wildlife experts cannot confirm that bears engage in such behavior. Biologist David Graber, who works in the Sequoia and Kings Canyon National Parks, even considers the vocal abilities of brown and black bears to be "quite limited, as befits a non-social animal." He distinguishes among five types of bear sounds. These include a "roar," produced when a bear is fighting another bear, or when a trained bear is coerced into some action. Black bears in particular tend to utter a "moan" or "sigh" when they are frustrated or unhappy. With a very deep, swallowing sound originating far back in the throat, a mother bear tells her cubs to slip away quietly from danger, but if she clicks her teeth the cubs know to climb a tree or otherwise flee as quickly as possible. Finally, bears make popping and blowing sounds with their mouths to frighten off people or other animals.

Naturalist and hunter Benjamin Kilham, who lives in the woodlands of New Hampshire, has taught and nurtured orphaned black bear cubs for many years and has developed a wider list of sounds, each one of which he associates with particular emotions and states of mind. His practices of intimately observing bears have sparked controversy, because he breaks with the common orthodoxy to minimize human contact.

BEARS—WHICH HAVE A great culinary interest in honey and bee larvae—react immediately to the humming of bees. They have even been known to confuse the vibration of telephone lines with bee sounds. Brown bears have destroyed a number of telephone poles in Siberia in their search for beehives they thought they heard at the tops of the poles. Smells also play a significant role in the lives of bears, as they are able to send olfactory messages to other members of the bear population. Odors from urine, feces, and body scent

Climbing after a honeycomb.

can identify an individual, divulge its sex or age, or indicate whether it is sexually receptive. Males use their urine to advertise their presence during the mating season to attract females and to warn other males.

Bears can also communicate with each other by marking trees with their scent. This is usually done by standing on their back legs and rubbing the back, shoulders, and especially the back of the head on a tree, telephone pole, or other object. They may bite and claw the trees, too. Any bear that passes a marked tree is almost certain to stop and smell it and perhaps add its own scent. Favorite marking places are often human-made signposts, many of which are shorter than the bears. There continue to be several competing theories regarding the significance of these markings. Ernest Seton-Thompson was among the first to voice the opinion that bears exhibit such behavior in an attempt to mark their territory. Enos Mills contradicted this view by stating that the meaning of these marked trees was purely informational, indicating a deer crossing or watering hole.

Unlike female bears, whose cubs remain with them for two to three years, male bears spend most of their lives alone. As the bear's mating period rarely lasts longer than two weeks, bears are truly—despite the incongruence of the name— lone "wolves." Furthermore, they undertake journeys that vary in length from weeks to months. Their keen senses, however, guarantee that they are aware of the presence of others of their kind, even though, unlike humans and many other mammals, they do not seek proximity to them. The scratch marks and scents they leave seem to satisfy their need to communicate with one another.

New Hampshire naturalist Benjamin Kilham has developed his own model of bear behavior. Despite the generally accepted view of bears as nonsocial animals, he has come to see them as animals who have developed complex marking systems and means of cooperating even with unrelated individuals to signal the presence of food. Even when there are fights over scarce food resources he sees principles of "fairness" in play, because in these cases harm, if inflicted, is not fatal and is usually limited at worst to severe wounds. In addition, Kilham sees bears and humans sharing basically the same drives and motives, and he favors the view of a converging evolution of different species who, by way of their existence at the same place and time, develop similar properties. For him, this explains—despite vast differences in terms of DNA—the strong ties between humans and bears.

Bears seem to like to travel in the footsteps of other bears: Russian bear researcher Aleksandr Fyodorovich Middendorf (1815–1894) discovered a chain of such imprints made from thousands of paw prints that stretched over hundreds of miles. The path created the impression that a dense population must be present even in the most remote forest areas. William Bingley documented a similar phenomenon in the American wilderness. He cited a report from someone named Düpratz, who once followed such a path for some time in the mistaken belief that it must have been created by human travelers, despite the fact that he was a good two hundred miles from any settlement. When he finally inspected the path more closely, however, he realized that the footprints were shorter than a human foot and that he could make out the imprint of a claw at the end of every toe. Unfortunately, Bingley does not tell us what Düpratz's thoughts were at this moment of realization. Did he pause to consider the weight of his discovery—or simply take to his heels in the opposite direction?

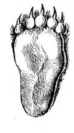

GIVEN BEARS' ACUTE senses, it is interesting to consider how the presence of humans might influence bears' behavior. A group of scientists from different European countries has recently investigated patterns of brown bear activity in the Dinaric mountains of Slovenia and Croatia, an area where bears are hunted between the fall and spring according to a quota system. By comparing the behavior of younger and older bears, the researchers found out that the latter have become predominantly nocturnal and very shy. Since almost all human activities, such as hunting, are conducted during the day, this behavioral shift is probably a response to the human activity. North American studies have also shown that

where humans are scarce or do not act aggressively, bears are largely diurnal or even give up
nocturnal habits they may have previously acquired.

THE NURSERY.

CHAPTER EIGHT

# Bears as Pets

Bears have never been domesticated—or have
they? An issue of *Harper's New Monthly* from
1856 includes an illustration of a mother with
two babies and two bear cubs. These are genuine, living bears, frolicking in a crib with a child.
What should we make of this picture? Upon reflection, this seemingly pleasant domestic idyll
reveals a cruel reality, since the cubs obviously
did not simply happen upon this family scene. In
fact, it was once popular to take in bear cubs
whose mothers had been killed in the hunt. People in the eighteenth and nineteenth centuries
seemed to have enjoyed the company of these
amusing, fur-covered, wild "little people," who
could serve as droll counterparts to their own
children. This resemblance to our own young
surely explains at least part of the bear's fascination for us.

That bears sometimes take on the role of "best
friend"—or that this relationship may be taken to
disturbing lengths—is not a development confined to America nor to recent centuries. One of
the earliest pieces of evidence is a brief account
by Roman philosopher Seneca (ca. 4 B.C.–65
A.D.), who told of bears that lived with humans
and allowed themselves to be petted. In his *History of the Northern Peoples,* the Swedish prelate

Bear cubs in the
nursery.

Olaus Magnus (1490–1558) even reported that Russians and Lithuanians knew how to put bears to work: Magnus claimed that at court bears were used alone or in groups to turn wheels that pumped water from deep springs, and that, standing upright, they hauled sacks of goods and loads of wood. Bears, he further asserted, were often placed as guards before the doors of the homes of rulers to ensure that no dangerous animals entered the premises. While adult bears are thus portrayed as threatening, Magnus considered cubs to be "wonderful, harmless playmates for children."

Bear, dog, and monkey as talismans in the Wild West.

Physician and world traveler Engelbert Kaempfer (1651–1716) observed that bears in Persia were smaller than those in Europe and were easy to tame. He described two bears that walked about unattended in the city of Isfahan, claiming that the duo would bother people who were eating lunch until they managed to get something for themselves. Because the animals belonged to the king, however, no one was willing to drive them away.

Bears powering a waterwheel.

According to scientist Georg Wilhelm Steller (1709–1746), the world's gentlest ursine inhabitant was the black bear of Kamchatka, a volcanic peninsula in northeastern Siberia, which is located across the Pacific Ocean from Alaska. On his Great Northern Expedition of 1733 to 1743, which he recounted in a book of the same name, Steller witnessed the Kamchatka bears running "in herds" and entering residents' houses. But this description, however remarkable, does not indicate that these bears actually lived together with humans.

Every traveler to this part of the world during this time seems to have contributed new information—some credible, some not—about mysterious contacts between humans and bears. Sometimes, as in the case of Swedish geographer Philip Johan von Strahlenberg (1676–1747), these accounts amounted to little more than hearsay. Strahlenberg acknowledged reports of people at the mouth of the Amur River in eastern Siberia "who tame bears and use them as we do horses." And in the middle of the seventeenth century Polish author Adam Kamiénski-Dłużyk ascribed similar talents to the Gilyaks, claiming that "they ride bears which they direct just as we direct horses, but they trim the animals' claws, remove their teeth, feed them in stalls like oxen and even eat them." The likelihood that this story is probably a mere fiction is attested to by a similar story of the Gilyaks themselves. One of their legends, an account of twin brothers who brought their bear cubs along whenever they went hunting on their skis, contains the recurring motif of reining bears, like huskies, to a sled. Once they grew larger, the story relates, the cubs were set to work pulling a sled themselves. Why did Western travelers never report witnessing such ursine talents directly?

The descriptions from the pen of J. A. Alexejenko seem more credible. In the early 1960s, the Leningrad cultural anthropologist wrote about the Kets, one of the smallest ethnic groups in western Siberia. For the Ket people, a bear was a sort of hairy wild man who was covered in fur in the same places that humans covered themselves with clothes. If they encountered a bear in the woods they would try to persuade him to do them no harm. "Go away, old man, I haven't done anything," is the bear-pacifying formula Alexejenko cited from a popular Ket story. He further claimed that childless couples were especially likely to raise bear cubs, living and eating with their foster "children" in one tent and even giving them real beds in which to sleep. According to Alexejenko, the owners talked with their bear charges, hung copper earrings in their ears and necklaces—a larger one each year—around their necks, and put bracelets around their paws. The neighbors were also happy to care for such "bear children." As they grew older, the bears were taken along on the hunt since their ability to smell the proximity of their wild relatives was a great help to their masters. Once they reached the age of three, Alexejenko wrote, the now-adult bears were set free in the taiga, still wearing their jewelry to show that they were not to be hunted.

A report by natural history writer Anton Benedikt Reichenbach showed that bears fed by humans in the Ural Mountains sometimes adopted not only the local preference for bread and potatoes but the bad habits of their benefactors as well. Reichenbach, writing in the mid-nineteenth century, recounted the story of a bear that wandered freely through the village and was "a lover of brandy." It apparently spent most of its time in the tavern, where visitors enjoyed getting the animal drunk.

The Ainu, in turn, are reputed to have had a particularly intimate relationship with bears: in fact, an old tradition even says that this group of people are descended from them. The Ainu inhabit the island of Hokkaido in the far north of Japan as well as Russia's (formerly Japanese) Kurilen archipelago and Sakhalin peninsula. For them, bears were disguised mountain spirits who entered our world to supply mankind with fur and meat. Their bear hunts ended with a festival to return the bear's soul so that he could intercede with the spirits for mercy and the people's future well-being. In addition to hunting the animals, the Ainu also captured cubs and kept them until adulthood in cages made from tree trunks. One aspect of the Ainu's dealings with bears, however, has tended either to disturb folklorists or to be dismissed by them: in Ainu traditional society the women were responsible for raising the bears they captured. Ainu women, who sported beard-like tattoos around their lips and on their cheeks, cared for the animals with great patience and also frequently nursed them—a practice that was not at all "secret," despite German religious historian Johann Jacob Bachofen's claim to the contrary in 1863. Although he apparently believed that this behavior should be kept under wraps, Bachofen had a great deal of sympathy for the Ainu women. "These bear lovers are not some sort of coarse, wild tribe," he assured his readers. "To the contrary, they distinguish themselves from the women of neighboring peoples through their morality, their tendency to gentle kindness, and their sense of honor."

The Ainu are not the only women said to have nursed bear cubs. Samuel Hearne, who from 1769 to 1772 traveled from Hudson Bay across the American Northwest to the Arctic Ocean, reported that "it is common for the Southern Indians to tame and domesticate the young [bear] cubs; and they are frequently taken so young that they cannot eat. On those occasions the Indians oblige their wives who have milk in their breasts to suckle them."

Ainu woman nursing a bear cub.

Women nursing animals is, from an anthropological point of view, not at all unusual: the women of some indigenous South American peoples, for example, are known to breastfeed small monkeys, a practice that is attributed to the

A captive bear drinking from a large bottle held by an Ainu tribeswoman.

fact that the monkeys play a vital role in their so-cieties—in fact, some of them even have quasi-human status. Similarly, bear cubs taken into the homes of various peoples of the Northern Hemi-sphere were considered members of the family and playmates for the children—at least until the cubs began to bite. Some households even went so far as to remove the bears' fangs and file their claws, which would buy the families a little more time with the bears.

In 1868, writer Julius Zähler, in a book on zoo-logical gardens, recommended that those who keep bear cubs observe certain rules: "Even when such a fellow is oh-so-tame and your good friend, he must never be allowed to lick you, for he will lick so long that the skin will begin to bleed, and once he has tasted blood he would rather have meat with it instead of keeping his best friend."

No matter how appealing the thought of raising cubs might be, the practice certainly did not make the bears' later adult lives easy. The passionate hunter A. Krementz, a careful observer of bears in Russia, was clearly familiar with this problem. In his study of bears, one of the few German books of the nineteenth century dealing exclusively with this animal, Krementz described the difficulties of persuading bears that their company was no longer appreciated. "Three six-month-old bears who had just been put out in a sack," he wrote, "found their way home through over three miles of swamp and water and expressed their happiness at arriving early the next morning by shattering the windows and, roaring with contentment, making their way to their old, familiar bed." He reported a similar story from a "professor" at the so-called Bear University in Smorgon, a town between Vilna and Minsk. The animals there were trained to do all kinds of tricks—dancing in couples, pushing baby carriages, and so on—before they underwent a "final examination" in front of a committee and were sold throughout the world. The bear trainer reported that one of his "black students," which he had presented as a gift, returned "from a place eight hours distant" in order to "complete his studies in the fine art of dance."

Swedish physician and writer Axel Munthe related another story of a supposed "house-bear." A woman in Norway, Munthe claimed, had raised a young bear that had been found in the forest. Even as an adult, the bear remained tame, would play with dogs and children, and was tied up only when the woman would visit her sister. One day the bear came running up to her as she walked through the woods on one of her visits. "He's gotten loose," the women thought, "and even lost his collar." Annoyed, she yelled at him to go home and threatened him with the umbrella she was carrying. When the bear hesitated, the woman became even angrier and hit him on the nose with her umbrella so hard that it broke in her hand. The bear ran off in the direction from which it had come. When she returned in the evening and saw the bear squatting dejectedly before the cottage, she began to reprimand it again, but the cook insisted that he had remained quietly tied up all day.

It is unlikely that bears are actually emotionally attached to their owners. Most likely they just want to be fed from a familiar hand—after all, bears raised by humans know nothing about searching for food in the wild. Such bears probably associate the scent of their caretakers with food their whole lives.

These accounts not only demonstrate that people and bear cubs have had astoundingly close relationships, they also reveal the limits of this intimacy. In 1857, for example, German professor Johann H. Blasius wrote that "bear cubs are easily tamed. They remain quite harmless until they are grown and become entirely used to their environment. Once they reach the age of four, however, they acquire a grimmer character, and these friendly relationships are usually destroyed by a violent outburst of the bear's true nature." For the Ainu and Gilyaks, taking leave of the bear occurred in the form of a bloody ritual. In societies in which bears were not so bound up with religious beliefs, they were simply put out or killed.

As far as we can judge from the few existing written records, the inhabitants of eastern Siberia seem to have come closest to domesticating bears. German cultural anthropologist Leo Frobe-

A bear cub and its "parents."

nius (1873–1938), who studied (among other subjects) African cults centered on the big cats, somewhat oddly referred to the bear-taming practices of the Gilyaks in his cultural history of Africa. Thanks to the skillful handling of the Gilyaks, he wrote, the bears among them "were as good as on their way to becoming pets." According to Frobenius, the fact that "the occasional taming of bears" did not become routine was due less to the bear's unsociable nature than to the animal's inability to breed in captivity. "And so," he concluded, "the summit of what could conceivably be achieved by this method remains out of reach, and the transformation suffices only to create a playmate for gypsies at the fair."

Once animals are truly domesticated, certain behavioral traits manifest themselves in their genes. Captive and seemingly "tame" bears have never undergone this transformation. For evolutionary biologist and historian Jared Diamond, the European brown bear's "nasty disposition" explains why this animal is "perhaps the most unlikely pet": "People have been killed by pigs, horses, camels, and cattle," he wrote. "Nevertheless, some large animals are more incurably dangerous than are others. Tendencies to kill humans have disqualified many otherwise seemingly ideal candidates for domestication." One obvious example of such a recalcitrant "ideal candidate" is the grizzly bear, which

Never more than a dream: bears as beasts of burden.

would be an excellent animal to raise for meat—if it would only behave in captivity. Of course, the very fact that brown bears eat meat, at least to a certain degree, would make them more challenging to keep than, let us say, sheep.

What sort of animals would live among us today had our ancestors managed to tame bears in the same way they did wolves? This is a fascinating question, but one that must remain forever unanswered.

NO ACCOUNT OF ATTEMPTS to domesticate bears would be complete without mentioning certain practices in Southeast Asia involving sun or Malay bears, animals just half the size of their American black bear cousins. In the wild, these bears inhabit the dense jungles from Indonesia in the south to the border of China and India in the north, but until recently they were still to be found at markets in places like the suburbs of Bangkok. These captive bears are doomed to live out a miserable existence in cages. No longer part of the gene pool, and cut off from the wilderness, they are essentially dead from an environmental perspective. Although killing animals violates the tenants of Buddhism, many of these bears end up in the kitchen, thanks to tourists who consider sampling bear meat—especially the paws—to be an essential aspect of their Asian vacations. Cases have even been reported of bears being dunked alive in boiling water like lobsters. During the subsequent feast, the livers are eaten raw, the blood drunk, and the meat grilled with sesame oil and chilies. The gallbladder, which many people believe to be a remedy for almost every disease and disorder imaginable, commands a high price. A lively business in bears once existed in places as far away as China and South Korea, but a number of countries in the region are taking measures to combat these practices. While such news is certainly reassuring, who can truly control what happens behind closed doors when good money from "gourmets" beckons?

# CHAPTER NINE

# An Observer in Eastern Siberia

The moon was shining the night in January 1856 when Leopold von Schrenck, a Russian-German zoologist, geographer, and cultural anthropologist, and Carl Maximowicz, his colleague and illustrator, reached Tebach, a village in easternmost Siberia. Von Schrenck was traveling in the name of the St. Petersburg Academy of Science, following in the footsteps—at least for a substantial part of the trip—of the great German scientist Alexander von Humboldt, who, almost three decades earlier, had made his way through the Baltic countries, Russia, and Siberia all the way to the Chinese border.

The Amur region is a barren area on the banks of the river of the same name that even today is known for its bears. They exhibit a variety of colorations, "from pure black and dark brownish black to pale brown," von Schrenck wrote in the first volume of his comprehensive report of his travels. Unlike their cousins on the volcanic Kamchatka Peninsula, which boasts a number of salmon-filled mountain streams, the Amur bears must rely entirely on the food they can scavenge in the forest. The Gilyaks and Mangoons, the region's inhabitants, informed von Schrenck that, as a result of this dearth of food, the bears were not as good-tempered as those on Kamchatka.

Inside the tent of the Gilyaks.

Hunger would sometimes drive them even to attack humans.

In Tebach, von Schrenck became one of the few Westerners to participate in a bear festival. The excitement of the Gilyaks was palpable, and von Schrenck could already hear their "loud cries of jubilation" while he was still some distance from the village. All the inhabitants were out and about when he arrived. It must have been a remarkable scene: the women, with babies in their arms, stood in front of the houses and watched as the men and the older children held hands and spun rapidly in a circle in a dance. Many of the participants kept slipping on the icy ground, and von Schrenck reported how the women "voiced their enthusiasm at every opportunity by screaming wildly in unison, stamping, and pounding loudly on their furs and skirts." Once the dance had ended, von Schrenck accompanied the group into a yurta, a kind of oversized tent. Inside, three bears were bound to the structure's two central support poles. The smallest was light brown in color, the largest dark brown, and the medium-sized almost black. Each had a thick leather strap around its neck and another around its back, and the two straps were knotted together to prevent the collar from slipping over the bear's head. The bears had room to lie down, stand, and move from side to side, and von Schrenck had to take care "to not be struck by a bear's paw." Despite the close quarters in the tent, the celebration continued: two villagers swung a rope and the others took turns jumping over it.

Finally the bears were untied and led from house to house. "The two men on each side of the bear had put on their furs inside out and tied their sealskin aprons as tight and flat around their bodies as possible, so that when the bears scratched at them their claws did not catch anywhere, but rather simply slid away on the smooth fur. . . . The train lurched along to the angry roaring of the bear that was being pulled back and forth, to which the other two animals soon joined in, and to the wild, wavering cries of the bear drivers and spectators—all moving forward and then falling back again, but gradually approaching the door of the house."

The ceremony lasted until the following morning, when the bears were brought back to the yurta where the entire production had begun. After the village dogs were fed, the bears were again led around the entire day. "As part of one or the other series of bear drivers, each individual had a chance to demonstrate his daring, courage, grace, and presence of mind; the closer he let the enraged animal approach him, the greater the ovation and thus his fame and the admiration he enjoyed among the people." This entertainment lasted for several days, occasionally interrupted by dog races, drumming by the women, and games.

At the same time, the place where the bears would meet their deaths was being prepared. Out in the open, a long rectangle was marked with poles, and two posts were rammed into the ground. The evening before their death, the bears were led onto the frozen surface of the river by the bright light of the moon: "It was a long train that set off to the stream, since besides the three bears, which were led in the same order as always, a number of unoccupied boys followed. As the bank is high and descends quite steeply to the river, it was interesting to see how the train moved down the slippery slope without becoming disordered, even for a moment. While those holding the forward rope ran down, those at the rear had to hold back with all their might to prevent the bear from rushing down just as quickly and causing damage. With their combined strength, they managed to bring all three bears to slide slowly and steadily down the slope." The way back was much less strenuous, however, because the bears pulled them back up the bank.

Throughout the night, the men fed the bears and paraded them about the village while the women prepared dishes for the next day's feast. No time remained for sleep. In the morning the bears were led once again to the river and then taken to a spot with a row of stakes, and each bear was tied to one of them. A short feast ensued, and then the entire village community gathered by the bears. Von Schrenck observed some of the men carrying regalia of a most peculiar kind: fir tree saplings whose branches—except for those at the very top—had been removed and a squirrel- or foxtail attached in their place. Placing these "banners" in front of the bears was the signal to untie them. One last time, the bears were led to the river and back. When

they returned, the village boys shot them with arrows, and the bears' owner decided which of the
boys should deliver the death blow. The carcasses were then dragged into one of the houses
and butchered. The villagers ate the meat and fat
throughout the remaining weeks of the festival,
and the three heads and the skins were hung on a
beam across from the yurta. "It thus appeared
that the bears had entered this dwelling and were
looking out of the window openings; the largest
in the middle, the smallest to his right and the
middle bear to his left—in other words, in the order they were kept earlier in the house," von
Schrenck wrote. Later, the heads and skins were
passed back into the house through the window
and placed on a bench reserved for the elders.

On a subsequent day bands on which toads

View of the
frozen river.

were depicted were tied around the bears' snouts in order to, as von Schrenck reported, "dry the tears welling from their eyes." The Gilyaks considered toads to be evil spirits and held them ultimately responsible for the fact that the bears had been captured, killed, and eaten. A second band of agate beads from China was then tied crosswise on the bears' heads. Von Schrenck saw in the placement of the beads on the bears' foreheads a parallel to the raised areas on the foreheads of certain Buddhist deities.

Contradictory attitudes toward bears seem apparent in the symbolism of the bear festival. Von Schrenck attempted to reconcile them by claiming that the festival was "partly motivated by the desire to honor a powerful predator and partly by superstitious fear of him and his revenging spirits. He is granted the place of honor in the house and the impression is created that the participants act both with his permission and against their will. In the end, they deflect all guilt and responsibility from themselves."

DESPITE VON SCHRENCK'S extensive observations and detailed records, all of which point to the intimate spiritual bond the people felt toward the bears, the Gilyaks kept some aspects about this peculiar relationship to themselves. This may be at least partly the result of the difficulty of finding an appropriate means to communicate their beliefs to foreign visitors. In any case, the ritual the scientist witnessed, one that has long since disappeared, not only challenges our feel-

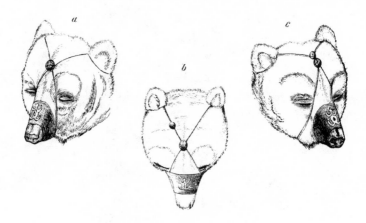

ings but presents us with a number of riddles. For example, von Schrenck did not directly observe what occurred during the feast and what was done with the bears' bones because, he wrote, these procedures "were undertaken in secret, or at least not in the presence of strangers."

Bear heads with amulets.

# CHAPTER TEN

# Face to Face

"Many of the eastern and western provinces are infested with them equally as much as with tigers," wrote Thomas Williamson, an official of the East India Company, as he described the Indian Bengals and the presence of bears there in the early nineteenth century. "To the east of the Ganges and Megna they are very numerous," he continued, "and on the western frontier, Rogonautpore may be considered their principal station. In marching through that country I scarcely ever missed seeing one or more daily, without deviating from the main road."

For many of us, simply seeing a bear at the side of the road would qualify as a memorable experience. But what would it be like to encounter one up close? The idea of coming face to face with such a powerful animal—or even testing our strength against it—holds a particular fascination for many commentators. In his book *Oriental Field Sports,* Williamson related the story of one such remarkable struggle: A gentleman was being carried to Mindapore in a *palankeen,* a carrier with a bamboo roof, when the bearers suddenly dropped their load and scattered in all directions. In short order, a half-grown bear climbed into the palankeen with the traveler, who had little choice but to fight the aggressive

Surprised by a hunter (1854).

animal. The bearers, in the meantime, had found hiding places from which they could observe the goings-on. The Englishman and the Bengal bear were now embroiled in a regular brawl. Each time a combatant gained the upper hand, the spectators responded with applause or a hearty cry of "Wau! Wau!" If the man gained control of the fight, they added "Sawbash saheb," which, Williamson noted, means something like, "Well done, Master!" If the bear seemed to be winning, however, they would yell "sawbash bauloo," ("Well done, Mr. Bear!"). The fight raged back and forth for some time, until the gentleman, who was seriously injured, managed to strangle the bear with his hands.

Williamson then related that the bearers hurried over, congratulated the victor, and continued the journey. Upon reaching the next stop, however, they were arrested because they had not helped to drive the bear away and, as was typical in India during this period, were led to the marketplace to be punished. The spectators, Williamson tells us, cried "sawbash sahib" whenever the whip met its mark and "sawbash bauloo" when the negligent bearers managed to avoid a blow. Years later, the gentleman would still tell the story of his fight with the bear to anyone who asked why his face was disfigured.

At about the same time, on a distant continent a large delegation was making its way on a journey of discovery from the mouth of the Missouri River to the Pacific Ocean—the famous expedition of Lewis and Clark. No such trip through the

wilderness would be complete without a bear encounter, and one of their companions indeed reported that he ran into a "white bear" outside the
camp one day. His horse was so frightened that it
threw the man, who landed at the bear's feet.
Since he was too close to the animal to shoot it,
the intrepid explorer hit it over the head with his
rifle. The bear was stunned for moment, giving
the man the chance to escape up a nearby tree.
After connecting with the bear's skull, however,
the rifle was now jammed, and he was forced to
wait on his uncomfortable perch for three hours
until the animal moved on. Only then could the
hapless adventurer climb back down, retrieve his
horse, and ride back to the camp.

Even more densely populated Europe could
serve as a stage for hair-raising bear encounters.
In Switzerland, in Hilterfingen on Lake Thun, a
strong man and a "grape-craving bear" encountered each other on a steep overhang in a vine-
yard. At least, this is the story as Carl Howard
(1796–1869), a local pastor, related it: "The bear
stood up, and the caretaker rushed toward it,

Finding refuge in
a tree.

wrapped one arm around the bear's neck and the other around its body, and pressed his head against that of the bear. The combatants remained motionless for a while, until one or the other became impatient with standing in this awkward position. The two then began taking small steps from side to side in order to find firm ground and, like wrestlers, choose a propitious moment to throw their opponent. Suddenly, however, one of the two stumbled over the edge of the overhang, and their arms were wrapped so tightly around each other that they both fell. Still clinging to one another, they rolled abruptly over the railing onto the path below. Half stunned from their rolling fall, they finally let go, both delighted to emerge unscathed from this unexpected bout of acrobatics. The bear climbed back up the incline, while the man followed the path home. He arrived in a condition far from normal, with a look of terror on his face and a mighty shaking in his limbs."

When hunter A. Krementz encountered a large brown bear deep in the Russian forest in the summer of 1872, he did not flee but instead intentionally drew nearer. "Master Bear," he reported, "was not the least bit disconcerted. He continued walking on serenely, stood for a while in the middle of the road, and then laid down and began contentedly rolling about in the sand. Suddenly, he got up again, shook the dust from his fur, gave me the once-over, let out a short roar, turned and went on his way, glancing now and then with disdain or mistrust in my direction." Krementz concluded that a bear will "never back down," claiming that "this is the guiding principle that defines its entire life and determines all its behavior."

Despite the vivid picture Krementz painted of the disdainful bear, determining a bear's state of mind from its facial expression is close to impossible. Aside from reptiles and most types of birds, bears are among the least expressive of land animals. The bear's largely immobile face remains a mask to human observers, revealing little about the animal's mental state. Only movements of the bear's ears, eyes, and highly flexible nose offer clues to its mood—attentiveness, interest, or fear. Although the bear gnashes its teeth as a threat, like other predators do, it does not confront its opponent with the "crescendo of hissing" typical of the cat species, and its stump tail limits the vocabulary of gestures the bear can perform with this—for many other animals—expressive appendage. This relative lack of facial animation could be a reason why bears are often considered sly and devious—no matter what they are up to, their faces look composed. A noticeable change occurs only when the animal opens its mouth to yawn or roar, and it is rare for it to bare its teeth. Furthermore, individual animals of the same species can usually be distinguished only by their size or typical behavior.

According to popular belief, bears possess not only great strength but a distinctive fighting style. Many accounts claim that the bear can seize its human opponent in a proverbial "bear hug" and crush him to death. Swiss hunter and naturalist

Playful fight.

Friedrich von Tschudi supplied one such account. He warned that bears can be dangerous if they are wounded, hungry, or suddenly awakened, or if their cubs are threatened. In such situations, Tschudi wrote, the bear "strides up to the enemy on its hind legs, wraps its arms around the foe, and tries to crush him." One hundred years later, in 1826, American naturalist John D. Godman described a man who was squeezed and almost suffocated in a fight with a bear. Should his readers find themselves in the same situation, Godman recommended, they should induce a spasm in the animal by pressing firmly with their fingers and thumb into the bear's neck at the point corresponding to the base of the tongue.

Surprisingly, bears that were taught the "humorous" art of boxing or wrestling with humans are not reported to have attempted squeezing their opponents. In any case, a mere blow from an angry bear's powerful paw would suffice to drive its claws into the body of its hapless foe.

After the "bear hug," one of the most enduring claims about bears is that they relentlessly pursue hunters who have shot them. Tschudi claimed that bears in the Carpathian mountains would follow hunters who had wounded them day and night, from forest to forest and from cliff to cliff, even swimming after them across streams. Furthermore, Tschudi wrote, the bears persisted for hours, searching caves, hiding places, and entire districts until they found and killed their attackers.

ON THE EVENING OF August 13, 1967, two young women were killed about ten miles apart by different grizzly bears in Montana's Glacier National Park. Not surprisingly, the incidents—the first deaths from grizzlies in any U.S. National Park since 1916—unleashed a torrent of press coverage. A call even went out to exterminate all the bears in the nation's parks. Both bears, it was determined, had habitually searched dumps and trash cans near camping spots for leftover food, and one would even eat from visitors' hands. As a result, the animals had apparently lost their fear of humans. In his account *The Night of the Grizzlies,* Jack Olsen calculated the probability of such a double attack as on the order of one in a trillion.

Not only did both attacks occur on the same day, but further investigation revealed that both victims were menstruating at the time they were killed. As a precaution, the authorities printed an informational brochure warning female visitors from hiking in areas where bears were present. A number of American biologists then took up the question of whether grizzlies were attracted by menstrual blood and if this could have played a role in the attacks.

Subsequent investigation failed to produce any evidence that bears were interested in human menstrual blood. Further studies followed. In one experiment, polar bears were presented with sea lion meat and tampons soaked with either menstrual or normal blood. The result: the polar bears were interested in the meat and the used tampons, but not those containing nonmenstrual blood. As a next step, black, Kodiak, and grizzly bears were offered the same three items, but each of these bears spurned the tampons entirely. The scientists then ascribed the polar bears' reaction to the menstrual blood to difficulties in adequately feeding the bears during the test, but continued to argue against lifting the warning. Statistics, however, offer no evidence that human menstrual blood interests bears. Yellowstone National Park had more than sixty-two million visitors between 1980 and 2002, during which time only thirty-two bear attacks were documented, and in twenty-five of these cases the victims were men.

If menstruation is not a factor, does gender itself play a role in the bear's choice of human prey? In the past, some scientists, including Theodore Zell and Gustav Jäger, argued for the existence of a "crossover rule," claiming that male animals were more likely to attack women (the question of whether the reverse were true—that is, whether female bears would tend to seek male victims—seems to have aroused less interest). Although this belief is reflected in the stories of many peoples, such as the Laplanders and the Buriates of Siberia, it remains unsubstantiated by scientific evidence.

If we were to rank worldwide locations where lethal conflicts between humans and various kinds of bears occur, the state of Madhya Pradesh in central India would be high on the list. Between 1989 and 1994, forty-eight people died there as a result of clashes with the shaggy, nocturnal, and relatively small sloth bear. No other animal in the region is the cause of so many injuries and deaths. Sloth bears in Sri Lanka show a similar penchant for violence, as the 1861 volume *Sketches of Natural History in Ceylon* attests. The sloth bear, Sir J. Emerson Tennent assured his readers, "evinces alarm on the approach of man or other animals and, unable to make a rapid retreat, his panic, rather than any vicious disposition, leads him to become an assailant in self-defence." The fact that the animal is simply afraid is cold comfort to the hapless individual under attack, however, since "so furious are his assaults under such circumstances that the Singhalese have a terror of his attack greater than that created by any other beast of the forest." The local inhabitants thus take the precaution of carrying a gun or "a light axe, called 'kodelly,' with which to strike them on the head," while "the bear, on the other hand, always aims at the face, and, if successful in prostrating his victim, usually com-

A sloth bear.

mences by assailing the eyes." The writer closes with a chilling pronouncement: "I have met numerous individuals on our journeys who exhibited frightful scars from such encounters, the white seams of their wounds contrasting hideously with the dark colour of the rest of their bodies."

Sloth bear attacks are in no way a thing of the past. In recent years, Sri Lankan wildlife expert Shyamala Ratnayeke has surveyed close to three hundred of her countrymen who have encountered and, in some cases, been injured by sloth bears. Most of these people earn their living from hunting and from collecting honey in the forest, activities in which they can all too easily surprise a sleeping bear. Those surveyed considered the bears' behavior to be aggressive, and they sometimes resorted to killing animals that attacked or threatened them. However, in the majority of cases they refrained from taking such drastic action. "The majority of respondents, surprisingly, supported legal protection of bears," the biologist reported, "and I found few signs of systematic culling and elimination of sloth bears. In the Western world," she concluded, "this animal would long since have been exterminated."

STEPHEN HERRERO, A Canadian environmental scientist and a leading scientific authority in the study of bear attacks, has collected a great deal of data for North America on this subject. He found that, between 1900 and 1980, at least forty-one people in North America were killed by bears. According to one of his more recent investigations, American black bears are known to have killed eleven people, and grizzly bears eight, during the first five years of the new millennium. Seven persons were killed by bears in 2005 alone. He relates the increase in fatal attacks to the fact that more and more people are active in bear habitats. Given that an estimated nine hundred thousand black bears live in North America, as opposed to only sixty thousand grizzlies, the latter clearly are much more dangerous to humans. His studies have also shown that most serious or fatal American black bear attacks are committed by male bears and are predatory in nature. In contrast, serious or fatal grizzly attacks are usually the work of females, apparently in defense of their young. Herrero believes that the different characteristics of attacks on humans by the two bear species correspond to differences in their evolutionary environments. In another study Herrero determined that polar bears have been known to have killed a human in Alaska only twice, a statistic that may simply reflect the fact that there aren't many polar bears there in the first place. Grizzlies, in turn, have been responsible for forty-five deaths in that state between 1900 and 2002—a figure that belies the popular belief that polar bears are the most dangerous bears of all.

Of course, many encounters or direct conflicts

between humans and bears go unreported or make only regional news. In 2005, the Minnesota Department of Natural Resources related that a fifty-year-old woman named Mary Munn encountered a black bear as she walked in the woods near her home, thirty miles south of Duluth. When the bear charged, Mary began to run but then stopped and turned to avoid being tackled from behind. The bear veered off but then charged again, and Mary responded by punching it repeatedly in the nose. Her dog managed to draw the bear away several times, but it always returned. At one point the bear clawed the woman's knee and she fell down. The bear bit her thigh and then clamped onto her armpit and began shaking her. Suddenly and inexplicably, however, the animal ran off, and Mary was able to walk home and call for help.

Although such reports can create the impression that bear attacks are a regular occurrence in small-town America, encountering a bear in the wild is no reason for panic. There are often no simple rules for acting under such circumstances, but the nature of a bear attack does depend on the species involved. Black bears (which rarely eat meat) are generally not aggressive, but inhabitants of North America are far more likely to encounter them than other kinds of bears. However, black bear attacks, while rare, do occur and are motivated by a predatory impulse: if a black bear is coming after you, it wants to kill and eat you. Author Nick Jans, who has a great deal of experience with bears, puts it like this: "Brown/

grizzlies are, far and away, the bears most likely to attack; black bears are almost always safe. Yet if a black bear does commit to an all-out assault, it's the ravening beast of nightmare." Herrero's findings also suggest that black bears are more likely to attack younger or smaller humans that appear more vulnerable. In any case, experts agree that if you are attacked by an aggressive black bear, you should fight back with all your might and with anything at hand—so Mary did the right thing by punching the bear in the nose. Trying to run is a mistake. Instead, you should do your best to drive the bear away—by shouting, throwing objects, or running toward it—before it really gets going.

The guidelines published by Denali National Park in Alaska for dealing with grizzly bears illustrate how differently animals of this species behave from their black bear cousins. According to the park's experts, the most serious mistake you can make with a grizzly is to encounter it by surprise, because it is precisely when they are startled that grizzlies find humans threatening and attack them. Since grizzlies can perceive human voices from a thousand feet away, they usually retreat long before a hiker draws near. Whistling, shouting, talking, or singing while hiking thus alerts them to your presence, even in areas where they might not see you otherwise or where the sound of running water can drown out your footsteps.

In the great majority of cases, the bears will go out of their way to avoid you. Dogs should be left at home, since they can track grizzlies and provoke them to aggression. Foods with strong odors such as fish, cheese, or raw meat should be carried in airtight containers and hung overnight well above the ground in bear-proof containers. You should stay at least fifty yards from any bears you do see, and twice that distance if cubs are present. If, despite these precautions, you find yourself face to face with a brown bear, the experts advise you to back up or make a wide detour. Do not draw nearer under any circumstances, no matter how tempting the opportunity seems—the photo of a lifetime could be the last one you take. Grizzly body language can provide valuable indications of the animal's mood. By standing up on its hind legs, the bear is not automatically demonstrating aggression—this posture is usually just a sign that the animal is interested in something. However, if it stands directly in front of you and roars or yawns, it is ready to attack, although its primary motive may be simply to defend its space. Resisting the impulse to flee is vital in this situation. Oddly enough, park rangers recommend lying face down on the ground with your arms around your neck and remaining still. This takes courage, but it is the best way to avoid a direct physical confrontation with a grizzly—a contest that humans are unlikely to win. If you think you are likely to need advice on this matter, you can consult the vast body of books on bear attacks and how to avoid them; this book is not the place for more detailed recommendations.

Before the thought of cowering face-down as a bear stands over you and sniffs your hair prompts you to cancel your Alaskan vacation, remember that you are unlikely ever to encounter a bear in the first place. Sensational reports of bear attacks may make for exciting reading, but they can easily create a false impression. For the most part, bears are far less interested in us than we are in them.

# CHAPTER ELEVEN

# Hunters and Hunted

It is impossible to know how many bears once lived in the primeval forests of Europe, Asia, and North America. But wherever and whenever humans and bears have shared the same space, it is the bears that were hunted and driven out—starting with the British Isles, where as early as around 1000 A.D. bears could no longer be found in the wild. In Germany and Switzerland, the bears vanished later in a sad process drawn out over the past five or six centuries.

Killing a bear was often considered proof of great courage, especially before the invention of firearms. Hunting was long a privilege reserved for the European aristocracy, a tradition that limited the number of hunters, but exceptions were sometimes made in the case of predators. Prizes were even offered to encourage commoners to hunt bears—and the bear, which was considered a threat, became the target of relentless pursuit. Hunters used large dogs to flush out the animals well into the sixteenth century and employed the "bear spear," a weapon with a six-foot shaft and a sharp and very pointed leaf-shaped blade, to deliver the death blow. To prevent the spear from penetrating too deeply into the animal's body, the weapon featured a bolt at the neck.

In the early part of the eighteenth century, the

Polar bear hunt (1854).

Bear hunt on Lake Koenig, Bavaria.

Swedish researcher Carl von Linné, better known to students of biology under the Latinized name of Linnaeus, traveled through the northern part of Scandinavia. He described how a Lapland hunter, aided by his dog, could hunt a bear. Linnaeus explained that a cord around the dog's jaws prevented it from barking and also served as a leash. "As soon as the dog smells the bear," he wrote, "he begins to show signs of uneasiness, and by dragging at the cord informs his master that the object of his pursuit is at no great distance." According to Linnaeus's account, the Laplander would remain downwind of the bear's hiding place as he advanced, "for otherwise the animal would by the scent be aware of his approach, though not able to see an enemy at any considerable distance, being half blinded by the sunshine." In this way, the hunter could draw near enough to shoot his prey, a feat "more easily accomplished in autumn, as the bear is then more fearless, and is continually prowling about for berries of different kinds, on which he feeds at that season of the year."

Linnaeus reminded us that the process was not without risks, however: if the hunter missed his target, the furious bear would attack before he could reload, forcing the "little Laplander" to flee. But the contest was not over yet—the hunter could win himself a second chance by dropping his knapsack on the ground as he ran. The bear would then stop to seize this prize, "biting and tearing it into a thousand pieces." At this point the hunter had "the opportunity of loading his gun, and firing a second time." Most of these second shots found their mark.

In eighteenth-century India, where the "entertainment value" of the hunt was especially prized, hunters would spear bears from horseback—a sporting amusement known as "bear sticking." Riding at full gallop through thick, high grass behind a pursued animal that, at any moment, could turn and attack horse and rider with razor-sharp claws, must have demanded a most particular acquired taste.

Although bears rarely attack humans without provocation, the bear hunt entailed a number of risks. A bear that had been shot or driven into a corner could turn on its attacker with all its might. In such cases, often the hunter's only chance was

Bear hunting in India (1807).

Knights fighting
with bears
(sixteenth
century).

to defend himself in close combat with a lance or knife. A catalog of "genuine secret hunting arts" from the early eighteenth century advised hunters to smear themselves with lion fat as protection from bears and wolves, since "as soon as they smell this, they flee." The uses for bears killed in the hunt were quite diverse, and, as far as we can reconstruct today, every bear-hunting culture had a unique approach for making the most of this prized kill. In vast stretches of Siberia, for example, the skin was used for mattresses, blankets, caps, gloves, soles of shoes, and collars for sled dogs. The fat and the meat were prized not only for their taste, but also for their supposed health benefits. Melted, the fat even served as a dressing for salads. The intestines could be fashioned into nearly transparent "windowpanes," and the shoulder blades became sickles for mowing grass.

Since bears travel on known paths, European hunters would set traps in particularly narrow passes, such as those in the Alps. They also made

*15.* **Wolf**, ⅔ nat. Gr.
*16.* **Hund.**
*17.Biber*, linker V. u. H. Lauf ⅓ n. G.

*18.Nerz,* l. H. L. ⅔ n. G. *19.Luchs.*
Sprungfährte. *20.Bär.*

Tracks in the forest. The bear's are on the right, second from the top.

use of gin and leg-hold traps, devices that caused the animals enormous suffering. No less perfidious were the slings attached to large stones placed by Siberian hunters in the Lena area. "As the bear majestically strides along, he catches his head and neck in the sling," reported natural

Polar bear hunt at night (nineteenth century).

history writer Anton Benedikt Reichenbach. "He looks around and angrily realizes that the heavy stone is hindering his progress. Then in a rage he climbs a peak, seizes the stone in his front paws, and throws it over the cliff. Of course the stone pulls the bear over with it."

Bears were also often killed in the winter by hunters who used dogs or smoke to frighten them out of their dens. Hunters in Poland and Russia, in turn, took advantage of the animal's proverbial sweet tooth. They left honey laced with alcohol for their quarry, which, upon consuming it, quickly became drunk and sleepy. In this state the animals could easily be captured or killed.

Swiss newspapers from the nineteenth century frequently reported on bears attacking, wounding, or eating sheep, cows, goats, or—far less frequently—horses in the Alps during the summer. In one account a bear is even said to have "restrainedly just sucked the blood" of its prey. The culprit was rarely caught red-handed but rather would leave a few telltale tracks at the scene of the crime. The obligatory hunting party to find the miscreant would quickly follow, but as many newspaper accounts further revealed, the supposed bear often turned out to be a "large dog" or other "black animal." Reports that humans met their deaths from bears are nowhere to be found. "The bear is apparently a virtuous animal that spares the lives of humans although they are his enemies," the Swiss newspaper *Bündner Tageblatt* concluded in 1866.

At that time, bear hunters enjoyed high social standing, and the hunt was not merely sport but part of a bitter daily struggle for survival. When—as was repeatedly the case in Switzerland in the early nineteenth century—the people suffered under famine, severe winters, or unseasonably cold summers, the loss of a single sheep could mean that a family would not survive the cold months. Of course, the assistance programs that farmers can turn to today were inconceivable then.

Bear making off with a piglet (nineteenth century).

During the second half of the nineteenth century, rear-loading firearms with greater precision became widely available, and killing bears became easier than ever before. This technological advancement helped to hasten the complete disappearance of bears from the Alps.

Swiss hunter and naturalist Friedrich von Tschudi believed that "the steepness of the crevasses, the danger of traveling over the snowless ground, the inhabitants' lack of interest and the scarcity of hunters" all were factors that would protect bears in less populated areas. Of course, Tschudi was dead wrong. By 1889, a satirical magazine asked whether the mountains would lose "part of their wonderful, mysterious

charm" when the bears were gone. "Why kill the educable and harmless bear, who is greedy, if at all, for calf or a cow? He should be tamed and employed as a tour guide—then all parties would benefit, and our Switzerland would again boast something novel and unique that diverges mightily from the same old bear hunts found elsewhere!" However we understand this satire, one thing is certain: the once clear consensus about bear hunting had begun to fray. Words like "beast" or "monster" appear less and less frequently in contemporary publications; instead, the bear is referred to affectionately as "Master Mutz" or "forest brother." At the beginning of the twentieth century, an increasing number of the Swiss began to call for a halt to the bear hunts. But such well-intentioned appeals for change came too late.

For Native American tribes, in contrast, the bear hunt was a sacred event that was accompanied by a number of rituals. As David Rockwell explained in *Giving Voice to Bear,* these rites were intimately related to the idea that bears were "among the most powerful of spirit helpers," and he noted that "shamanic healers and some of the bear societies drew on the bear's spirit power to effect cures." In some cases, this veneration was so great that the tribes—among them, the Navajo, the Pueblo, and Pima—abstained from hunting bears altogether. The Cheyenne considered bears to be their relatives and, not surprisingly, refused to eat them. They were not alone—most of the plains tribes and some in California avoided hunting the animals.

In the case of the Cree, an Algonquin-speaking group from northeastern Canada, the hunters' first task was to establish communication with the animals' spirits, which they imagined as a force distinct from the animals themselves. As Rockwell wrote, "The Cree believed that if they respected the animals they killed and observed all

Giatgen Platz Spegnas von Tinizong, Swiss bear and chamois hunter.

the taboos, the owners or keepers of the animals would be pleased and inclined to release more animals. Once free, the animals themselves could choose to be killed." Dreams helped to divine the outcome of a bear hunt and could tell the hunter where to find an animal in the first place. If such nocturnal auguries failed him, however, he could simply check old den sites. The Cree hunter then tried to lure the bear out, saying, "Grandfather, it is already warm! Time for you to come out now." The Cree considered only clubs, axes, or spears to be proper implements for killing a bear—bows, arrows, and guns were taboo. After a kill, the hunter would put a lit pipe into the dead bear's mouth and blow into it to fill the bear's throat with smoke—a procedure meant to calm the animal's spirit and prevent it from seeking revenge. Some hunters would also apologize to the bear or find a way to blame someone or something else for its death. In short, most Native American cultures sympathized with the animals they hunted.

European settlers, however, were not burdened with such respectful attitudes toward their prey. The chase for grizzlies in the nineteenth century unfolded at breakneck speed, and on an entirely different scale than the bear hunts of Europe. The farther that settlers penetrated the American West, the more bears became their targets, and when these settlers began raising cattle and farm stock their already negative perspective on bears took a dramatic turn for the worse. In Texas, for example, the number of cattle multi-

Hunting scene in Germany (1852).

plied from one hundred thousand in 1830 to more than three and a half million by 1860. This development was bad news for the abundant grizzly population—because the bears posed a danger to the valuable stock, killing them was considered good for business. Campaigns were organized regularly to stamp out the ursine vandals. Unlike the buffalo, another victim of nineteenth-century hunting fervor, the bear was not killed for its hide, meat, or tongue, but simply to protect economic interests. The introduction of high-powered repeating rifles further increased the number of bear hunters. Many of America's plentiful bear populations were wiped out: the last grizzly bear in Texas was killed in 1890, in California in 1922, in Utah in 1923, and in Oregon and Arizona in 1935. Yet despite the grizzly's lamentable absence from the wilds of California, it still occupies a proud position on that state's flag.

Although as a country the United States has earned the dubious honor of being among the bear hunting champions in the world—nowhere else have as many bears been wiped out in such a short amount of time—Russia has produced some amazing individual feats. In 1936 a one-hundred-and-ten-year-old man named Farkow, living in Krasnojarsk in eastern Siberia, was celebrated for having killed 138 bears during the course of his many years, including two he had strangled with his bare hands. By the time he was honored, however, the "bear killer" had already been retired for a decade, after deciding at the age of one hundred to devote all of his attention to fishing.

But the most gruesome record of all is attributed to his countrywoman, the elderly Elisaweta Butina from Vladivostok, who received the title "Great Huntress" on her eighty-third birthday, in the summer of 1937. This hardy Amazon is said to have killed her one thousandth bear shortly before her birthday, a feat all the more remarkable since she supposedly first took up hunting at the age of seventy. At that time she had suddenly felt threatened by bears on her small farm and had requested a firearm. Aided by a few assistants, she then crusaded unrelentingly against the "parasites" in the region, while—despite her age —rowing her own boat, catching her own fish, and mowing her own fields. She herself also skinned the bears she killed.

Such ruthless pursuit of these animals is fortunately a thing of the past, but bear hunting is still very much with us. It is an issue with the power to stir up strong emotions. The motives for and character of the bear hunt have changed substantially, though: in North America today, bears are hunted primarily as a leisure activity, not to fulfill essential needs or to prevent humans from harm. A search for "bear hunting" on the Internet turns up Web sites where enthusiasts exchange information about where and how to best hunt the animals. Uninitiated readers can find it unsettling to learn about "magnificent hunts where success is guaranteed" or to read reports of "helicopter hunts" on Kamchatka or "psychologically challenging" polar bear hunts in Canada—challenging not because the goal is to shoot these animals, but because the hunters see nothing but "endless white expanses" for days on end. Along with their stories, the proud hunters post photos of themselves with their spoils.

But whether nonhunters like it or not, this activity is always likely to draw a large and enthusiastic crowd. Bear hunting today is also far from the free-for-all slaughter that claimed the bulk of America's grizzlies. In the United States, for example, hunting black bears is now a strictly regulated activity. In addition to a basic hunting or sporting license, bear hunters usually must purchase a special permit, hunt the animals only during a defined period, and kill only a certain number of them.

Various methods exist for hunting black bears —bait, hounds, and artificial (or even laser) lights can be used. It is up to the individual states to determine which methods are acceptable. In Massachusetts, for example, baiting has been illegal since 1970, and hunting with dogs since 1996. Hunters are also not permitted to hunt bears "incidentally" during the firearms season for deer. Since the "shotgun" season begins after Thanksgiving, many of the animals have already retreated to their dens for the winter. As a result, hunters must either take a position on a stand in a likely feeding area—the method that accounts for most of the kills—or slowly stalk through the berry patches that attract their quarry. Hunters scouting for bears look for tracks, scat, or bedding areas, or for claw marks or "bear nests" in beeches. The bears may also leave well-worn trails in cornfields or in large patches of berry plants. Farmers planting fields of feed corn sometimes even permit hunting on their property.

A brochure from the Massachusetts Division of Fishery and Wildlife gives a sense of the thrill those susceptible to the attractions of hunting may experience. It admonishes hunters to "pay attention to the direction of the wind," stressing that "bears have a keen sense of smell and will quickly pick up on your presence." As a result, hunters are encouraged to "place yourself downwind when hunting and, if possible, come into your stand from a direction different from that used by the bears." They are also admonished to remain alert: "The bears blend in with the background very well, especially in early morning and evening. You can easily fail to see the bear if it crosses from woods to corn when you are dozing or looking the other way. Bears can move very quietly when they want to and you may not hear the animal coming. If you are alert and vigilant you have a better chance of scoring."

Most bears are taken with rifles, typically of the .30-06 type. A successful hunter must bring the entire animal to an official checking station within forty-eight hours of the kill. There a biologist will record certain information, weigh the bear, and remove a tooth to determine its age. The authorities stress that Massachusetts' black bear population is healthy and growing—hunting takes about 5 to 7 percent of the estimated population each year, while bear numbers continue to grow at a moderate rate—and that sportsmen play an important role in the animal's conservation and management.

DO HUNTING AND CONSERVATION always go hand in hand? Many wildlife activists were incensed when, at the end of 2005, the U.S. Department of the Interior and the U.S. Fish and Wildlife Service announced that grizzly bears in areas around Yellowstone National Park should no longer be considered threatened, arguing that the greater Yellowstone population of grizzly bears has recovered and no longer needs the protection of the Endangered Species Act. By the mid-1970s, guns, traps, poisons, snares, and the loss of habitat had reduced the number of grizzlies in the western United States from an estimated fifty thousand animals to fewer than eight hundred. Perhaps two hundred of these remaining bears lived in and around Yellowstone National Park. Like the survivors they are, the grizzlies held on, and now about twelve hundred of them live south of the Canadian border. More than half of them can be found in the Yellowstone ecosystem, centered around the park and six adjacent national forests, where the grizzly population has been increasing at the rate of 4 to 7 percent annually for at least the past fifteen years.

Those opposed to removing the bears from the list of endangered species object to putting the fate of these animals, many of which live outside the recovery zone, into the hands of states in which many residents are hostile toward bears. They fear that, if the protection of the government is removed, the states may reintroduce grizzly hunting seasons—and thus again allow the proud symbols of the American West to end up as stuffed trophies.

# CHAPTER TWELVE

# The Inuit and Polar Bears

While researching this book I came across Reverend John George Wood's old volume *Nature's Teachings,* which describes many examples of humans adopting the behavior of animals. Wood mentions two interesting cases to argue that humans learned seal-hunting techniques from polar bears. Because even at rest seals frequently lift their heads and scan the area for foes, they are difficult to approach, and so catching them is a challenge. The evidence for Wood's claim comes from a certain Captain Hall, who undertook an Arctic expedition in 1871. According to Hall, a hunting polar bear "proceeds very cautiously towards the black speck, far off on the ice, which he knows to be a Seal. When still a long way from it, he throws himself down and hitches himself along towards his game. The seal, meanwhile, is taking its naps of about ten seconds each, invariably raising its head and surveying the entire horizon before composing itself again to brief slumber." Hall goes on to describe a most curious scene: "As soon as it raises its head, the Bear 'talks,' keeping perfectly still. The Seal, if it sees anything, sees but the head, which it takes for that of another Seal. It sleeps again. Again the Bear hitches himself along, and once more the

The way to approach seals. Seal looks around, only to be 'talked' to and again deceived. Thus the pursuit goes on until the Seal is caught, or till it makes its escape, which it seldom does." Wood claimed that Inuit hunters used the same technique to catch seals, albeit with less success than their ursine role models. Their practices changed dramatically once they had access to white cloth shields for camouflage.

Wood's second example is even more astonishing: he claims that the "Esquimaux" copied a bear technique for catching adult seals by using the seals' young as lures. "When an Esquimaux hunter catches a young Seal," Wood wrote, "he takes care not to kill it at once, as he wishes to use it as a decoy." Wood further claimed that the hunter then "ties a long line round one of the hind flippers" (the bear, as we can see in the illustration, simply uses its paw) and "drops the little seal into the hole through the ice by which it enters and leaves the water." When the mother seal comes to the aid of her offspring, "the young seal

is cautiously drawn up on the ice" by the hunter. The anxious mother follows, "and, as soon as she is within reach, she is struck with the harpoon." Like most stories that sound too good to be true, however, this account is a pure invention.

Using decoys to catch seals.

WHEN FRANZ BOAS (1858–1941), the "father of American anthropology," wrote his 1888 landmark study *The Central Eskimo,* polar bear hunting had already changed in significant ways. "The chase of the musk ox and that of the bear have become much easier since the introduction of firearms in Arctic America," he wrote, "and the Eskimo can kill their game without encountering the same dangers as formerly." In fact, even though the Inuit Eskimos have interacted with the polar bear, or *Nanuk,* for millennia, considerable evidence exists that the bears played a minor role in the Eskimos' actual subsistence before the advent of firearms. Animal remains recovered from various Inuit sites almost never include those of polar bears: among the twenty-seven thousand bone elements that archaeologist Jeppe Møhl collected at Nurgarsak in West Greenland, a site believed to be representative for the ancient Thule Culture (1000–1600 A.D.), exactly five can be traced to these animals.

Nonetheless, it seems fair to say that the polar bear has historically occupied a very special place in the world of the Inuit. Among the Netsilik Eskimos, for example, the bear—like the seal or the caribou, which for them are the other most important other game animals—was embedded in a system of taboos and rituals, and it was believed to have a soul. "The soul of the bear was considered to be particularly dangerous and powerful, and numerous exacting observances were necessary to counter any revengeful intentions its soul might have had at the end of the hunt," wrote anthropologist Asen Balikci. Because the Netsilik thought that the soul of a slain bear "remained on the tip of the hunter's spear for four or five days," they undertook elaborate rituals "to avoid the soul's turning into an evil spirit." According to Balikci, "the skin had to be hung inside the house and surrounded by various implements, all man's or all woman's work was forbidden, including sledge shoeing, and presents to the soul of the bear had to be placed on its skin." The special fascination with the polar bear may also have to do with the fact that it moves as adroitly in the water as on land—the cosmology of the Netsilik strictly separated how land and sea animals should be hunted and their bodies eaten or used. As anthropologist Knud Rasmussen explained, "these observances were really ways to confirm symbolically the separation of the world into two halves: land and sea."

When the Netsilik encountered polar bears while traveling or hunting, ferocious battles often ensued. "First they let loose the dogs, who rushed madly at the bear, attacking it from all sides," Balikci reported. "The bear clawed viciously at the dogs, but they were quick enough to avoid his attacks and were able to keep the bear at bay until the arrival of the hunters." The hunters, in turn, used barbless harpoon heads specially adapted for spearing bears. Netsilik hunters could be horribly wounded in these dangerous fights, but they are said never to have withdrawn from a bear hunt. Boas offered similar descriptions of Inuit bear hunts, but he also related that, according to an unwritten law, "a bear or a young seal belongs to the man who first saw it, no matter who kills it."

For the Inuit, land and sea animals, snowstorms and thunder—in short, all elements of nature—were subject to the shaman's power. When game was unavailable, the shaman would be asked to use his spiritual abilities to learn where the animals could be found. In some cases, he would report that a breach of taboo had brought about the famine and direct the people to confess their wrongdoing. However, shamans could also use their powers for harm, and a special association existed between evil shamans and bear souls. "The Netsilik lived in perpetual fear of wandering animal ghosts, since they depended for survival on regularly killing animals," Balikci wrote. As a result, "the very food which was absolutely essential for the survival of society became a source of evil." The Netsilik therefore believed that a number of strange beings populated their country, including giant bears called *Nanorluk*. According to Netsilik legend, the jaws of a Nanorluk were so large that it could swallow a man whole. The unfortunate victim of the monstrous bear's taste for human flesh would suffocate in the bear's belly. On the other end of the spectrum, the Netsilik also believed in the existence of a race of dwarfs called *Inuarugligarsuit*. These miniature people supposedly resembled their human counterparts in every way and hunted correspondingly tiny versions of the same animals the Inuit themselves did, including bears no bigger than lemmings.

A CLOSER LOOK AT THE changes that have taken place since Boas made his observations reveals that a complex set of factors has a bearing on polar bears in Inuit areas today. Canadian geographer George Wenzel has emphasized that polar bears were first exploited economically after other sources of revenue for the local people dried up. In the late nineteenth century, the population of bowhead whales declined, leading to increased hunting of walrus and narwhal for their ivory. During the 1940s, more modern firearms became available to the Inuit, and bears started to play a more important role in the fur trade with Europeans. Hunting polar bears for sport became popular later.

With the passage of the U.S. Marine Mammal Protection Act and the Canadian Agreement on Conservation of Polar Bears in the early 1970s, the governments also recognized the needs of their Inuit citizens to exploit bears for economic subsistence. In the case of the Nunavut people, their Wildlife Management Board sets a yearly hunting quota. While this number was slightly above four hundred in 2002, just three hundred and eighty-five bears were actually killed. Most fell to local hunters, but sixty-nine were shot by foreign sportsmen, who paid about thirty thousand Canadian dollars or more apiece for the privilege. Wenzel has pointed out that the Inuit receive barely one-half of this money, but this nevertheless means that hunting is a source of considerable income for them.

The regulation of this activity demonstrates that responsible hunting can serve beneficial ends and that its economic impact on the Inuit culture would be difficult to replace. Surprisingly, although the Inuit are free to allocate the entire legal harvest of polar bears to lucrative sport hunting, they prefer to restrict the number of bears killed by foreigners to about a quarter of the total.

As Wenzel wrote, the priority the Inuit place on hunting the bears themselves shows that "the cultural value Inuit place on *nanuq* is decidedly more important than the economic return polar bears might provide."

The real threat to polar bears—and thus to the Inuit—comes from a different direction: their icy environs are shrinking. The loss of polar bear habitat because of global warming poses a far greater danger to the bears than hunters do. Every year, from October to January, hundreds of polar bears—the largest carnivores living on land—are on the move. After the lean summer months in the tundra, they hungrily eye the Hudson Bay, waiting for it to freeze over so that they can finally travel the pack ice in search of seals. But the winter comes later and later and the thaw earlier and earlier. As a result, little time remains for the bears to eat enough to rebuild the layer of fat that protects them from the cold and allows them to survive the winter months. On average, polar bears weigh almost two hundred pounds less than they did just fifteen years ago. Males today seldom reach their full possible weight of seventeen hundred pounds.

According to a recent study by the International Union for Conservation of Nature and Natural Resources, the combined effect of melting sea ice and overhunting could diminish the polar bear population by at least 30 percent in coming decades. This means that the world would contain very few polar bears: experts estimate that there are only about fifteen thousand left in Canada, and twenty-two thousand throughout the Arctic. The polar bear has thus become the symbol not only of Arctic vulnerability but of the ecological crisis of our planet.

CHAPTER THIRTEEN

# Closer Than Close

Cat lovers are the stuff of legend. Entire generations of French poets bore witness to the fascination cats hold for us. In contrast, bears—who, at
least as adults, do not admit such close contact—
inspire a more complicated relationship. Instead
of enjoying direct interaction, their admirers
must usually content themselves with a variety
of fetishistic substitutes—or settle for a so-called
bear in the form of a bearded, powerful man. Despite or, perhaps, because of their unattainability,
modern society yields plenty of interesting and
provocative attitudes toward bears that are ripe
for study by cultural anthropologists—and probably by psychologists as well.

But a few remarkable characters overcame the
considerable difficulties and were able to forge
close relationships with bears. One legendary
North American hunter and showman, for example, sought both physical contact and conflict
with these animals and thereby embodied the
contradictions in our dealings with them. Fortunately, his life is thoroughly documented—
partly by him directly and sometimes by others—although doubts as to the reliability of some
of these reports are certainly justified.

Grizzly Adams—for that is of course whom I
mean—was an eccentric loner and one of the

Grizzly Adams
and Ben Franklin.

most mysterious personalities of the already colorful Wild West. Born in Massachusetts as John Adams in 1812, he preferred to be known as William or James Capen Adams, even though the latter name already belonged to his brother. Others came to call him Old Adams or Bruin Adams. Although many a historian has wracked his brain in search of the reason Adams adopted these pseudonyms, the most likely explanation is that he just wanted to mark the start of a new life in the West.

At the onset of the California Gold Rush, Adams, a shoemaker by trade, left his wife and child behind and set out on his way. He supposedly traveled through Mexico to reach the Sierra Nevada. The wild landscape of California, with its high mountains, offered a stark contrast to his eastern home. Adams planned to prospect for gold while earning his keep as a shoemaker, but he had little understanding of the technical problems involved and was soon forced to leave his claim. From then on he wandered with a wagon through the mountains. He must have been a remarkable sight: with his long hair and beard, wearing a fur jacket and a cap decorated with a foxtail, he quickly became a sort of Robinson Crusoe of the Sierra.

Back in Massachusetts he had sometimes caught foxes, wolves, and wildcats in the forest and sold them to zoos. He now took up this business again, this time with other sorts of animals. Not only did he shoot grizzly bears and sell their meat and fur, but he also engaged in the more lucrative—and considerably more difficult—practice of catching bears alive with a lasso and selling them to the organizers of animal fights. "Next Sunday, the famous grizzly bear 'America' will fight a wild bull"—this or something like it would have appeared on posters for such an event.

Adams developed a special relationship with the region's native inhabitants, who were happy to have his well-equipped assistance when they were hunting with bows and arrows. To show their gratitude they helped him to tan animal skins, which he sold to prospectors, or they gathered grass that he could feed to his animals in the winter. In time Adams began to tame and display every imaginable sort of animal: deer, wolves, beavers, rabbits, minks—and bears. Grizzly bears presented a special challenge, one that Adams enjoyed. One cub, which he dubbed Lady Washington, won Adams's heart with her stubbornness: "I fell in love with the cub because she was so ill-natured. I felt a species of delight in subduing, little by little, a will so resolute and a temper so obstinate."

Adams was convinced that bears could be equally compatible as companions as dogs, and felt that his gradual progress in handling them justified this belief. George Washington and Buchanan, two black bear cubs, supposedly even slept with Adams at his fireside under a single blanket. Grizzly cubs, on the other hand, were difficult to tame. Even Adams considered them dangerous and always kept them chained.

His contact with the animals seems to have affected his own behavior. Legend holds that Adams, wrapped in a bearskin, once approached a sleeping Indian, who started upright, terrified. As the Indian reached for his weapon, Adams let out a threatening roar, which caused his unwitting adversary to drop everything and run away. But his fame is due to his performances of a more public nature. In the spring of 1853, Adams held a wrestling match with one of his bears in Mariposa and earned the considerable sum of eight hundred dollars. When he brought his menagerie into town the inhabitants were greeted with the sight of a kingly procession of twelve men, thirty-six horses, two mules, and various wild beasts— some running free and some bound to the pack animals.

With the stubborn determination he admired in his charges, Adams repeatedly tried to capture a giant grizzly. For this purpose he once built a "trap hut" the size of a small cottage. Adams and his assistants placed a freshly shot deer inside and then retreated to their posts to wait. When the bear finally appeared, Adams was speechless.

"He looked like a moving mountain," he recalled, "and my heart fluttered for fear of being discovered." But the giant simply remained standing in front of the trap. Adams tried every trick in the book to lure him in, but even a trail of sugar failed to work. One night he was awakened by a loud roaring—the bear had finally landed in the trap, but he struggled so mightily that the men feared he would escape. Two months passed before Adams could arrange for an iron cage that could transport the bear, which by this time had been named Samson.

Adams was lucky to escape with his life several times near the end of his hunting career. On one occasion he found himself in a match with a female grizzly and barely managed to limp away. He had shot the bear through the shoulder, whereupon she immediately attacked. Adams survived the resulting hand-to-hand combat when he was finally able to kill her with his knife.

In 1855, Adams and his train made their way to San Francisco, where he presented his animals in a dark, damp basement to an astounded public. Along with Ben, Lady Washington, and Samson, the menagerie featured seven other black bears. Journalist Theodore H. Hittell, apparently very much impressed by the show, left a detailed report for posterity. Adams, he wrote, was "quite as strange as any of his animals." The famous hunter was "a little over medium size, muscular and wiry, with sharp features and penetrating eyes." Hittell estimated Adams to be "about fifty

Adams and his animals parading through San Francisco.

years of age" despite his gray hair and white beard. He described his subject as wearing "a coat and pantaloons of buckskin, fringed at the edges and along the seams of the arms and legs," complemented by "a cap of deerskin, ornamented with a foxtail," and buckskin moccasins.

The reporter's enthusiasm also extended to the bears themselves, although his expertise in ursine matters left something to be desired. Despite the fact that Lady Washington had been captured in America, Hittell claimed that she was from Alaska—which in 1867 was still part of Russia. This "Russian bear" was, according to Hittell, "very savage" compared with "the grizzly, Ben Franklin" (Ben was actually a black bear). Hittell declared Lady Washington's cub to be "the president of the gathering," while the "star" was "Funny Joe," a two-year-old grizzly with a light-colored pelt who was "as playful and humorous as a monkey."

In 1860, Adams boarded a ship for New York.

He was already in poor health, and during the voyage one of his grizzlies is reported to have severely attacked him, reopening a nearly healed wound in his head. He lived another six months with his wife and daughter and worked for a short time with the showman P. T. Barnum, but he missed the West to his dying day. "I have attended preaching every day, Sundays and all, for the last six years," he said on his deathbed. "Sometimes an old grizzly gave me the sermon, sometimes it was a panther; often it was the thunder and lightning, the tempest, or the hurricane on the peaks of the Sierra Nevada or in the gorges of the Rocky Mountains, but whatever preached to me, it always taught me the underlying majesty of the Creator and revealed to me the undying and unchanging love of our kind Father in Heaven."

James Capen Adams died on October 25, 1860. *Harper's Weekly* glorified his unusual life: "His tastes led him to cultivate the society of bears, which he did at great personal risk but with remarkable success, using them as packhorses, by day, as blankets by night, as companions at all times." The report encouraged readers to remember how the remarkable fellow with the two bears would take a walk with his pets every morning down Broadway, accompanied by a drummer and a piccolo player. There was always the chance, the magazine reminded its readers, that Adams would pay for his daring with a leg, an arm, or even part of his head. The fact that

Grizzly Adams contributed to the bears' decimation—despite his "love" for them—remained unmentioned.

ABOUT A HUNDRED YEARS after Adams's death, another eccentric bear lover entered the scene. Timothy Dexter, who became better known by the name Timothy Treadwell, is as rooted in the legend of Grizzly Adams as he is a product of our contemporary world. Born, like Adams, on the East Coast—in his case in Long Island, New York, in approximately 1957—he claimed to have sensed a kinship with animals from his earliest days. A high school dropout, he headed to southern California and entered a world of punk rock, surfing, violence, and drugs.

In 1989 he set out on a motorcycle for Alaska, intent on seeing grizzlies. He met one in Wrangell-St. Elias National Park, a primal experience he later recalled in his book *Among Grizzlies.* "For me the encounter was like looking into a mirror," he reported. "I gazed into the face of a kindred soul, a being that was probably lethal, but in reality was just as frightened as I was." Similar experiences in other parts of Alaska convinced him that he had a special way with bears, and in one instance he even saw himself as a young bear's "adopted human companion."

Soon Timothy Treadwell devoted his life to bears and their preservation. Interestingly—and this is one of the many paradoxes about Treadwell—in Katmai National Park and Reserve, the area he frequented, bears were not endangered at all. In fact, the whole park has about three thousand of them. But Treadwell felt strongly that bears were misunderstood, and it became his mission to prove that they are essentially peaceful creatures that can get along fine with humans or even be their friends. He not only sought the animals' proximity wherever he could, but sang to them and even went so far as to imitate their movements and vocalizations. In short, he wanted to be one of them.

Starting in the mid-1990s, Treadwell spent more and more time at the Katmai coast, usually arriving in early June and staying until the end of September. Incidents such as a wounded bear sleeping for weeks near his tent, or a mother bear leaving her cubs nearby, encouraged him to believe that bears were peaceful creatures. When they did threaten him he would simply ignore them, and only once did he use the pepper-based bear spray he carried with him. He also didn't set up the portable electric fences bear researchers use to keep the animals at a safe distance and was even hiding his camp in dense thickets to keep it out of view of park rangers. With time, the media became interested in his story, and he was sought after for documentary and feature films, magazine articles, and appearances on talk shows like CBS's *Late Show with David Letterman*.

As Treadwell became better known to the public, wildlife experts increasingly spoke out against his methods. He was accused of blatantly ignoring the dangers of working with bears and, in turn, exposing the bears to risk by getting them used to humans and thus increasing the likelihood of dangerous human-bear encounters in the future. To some it didn't come as a surprise when a bear killed and partially ate Timothy Treadwell and his girlfriend, Amie Huguenard, on October 5, 2003, at the end of Treadwell's thirteenth season in Alaska. An audio recording that cuts off in the middle of Huguenard's high-pitched screaming survived the attack to document the horrific scene (but will not be released to the public). Treadwell's life and death were the subject of Werner Herzog's 2005 award-winning documentary *Grizzly Man,* which helped to make the story the most publicized bear attack in history. In the film Treadwell can be observed in several close encounters with bears, while talking in a soft, almost childlike voice.

Just a weird guy on all fours? Simply dismissing Treadwell as more or less disturbed, irresponsible, or lacking proper judgment is too simple. Although he was indeed incapable of drawing the boundaries necessary to protect his own life, his story is inconceivable if we disregard the longing for a kinship with bears and the wish to coexist with them peacefully that motivated him—a desire likely born from hearing a multitude of unrealistic stories about humans connecting with these animals. His conviction that it was up to him to save the bears must have also played a role, along with the wish to achieve a measure of fame and fortune, although the complex world of humans seems to have held little attraction for him.

We should also remember that we live in a time in which many people—often inspired by others' accounts of adventure and life on the edge—intentionally seek out extreme situations. By facing danger, they want to prove that any obstacle can be overcome by someone with whatever it takes, be it courage, perseverance, or empathy. All these impulses, and perhaps a few more, came together to produce the ultimately fatal obsession of Timothy (Treadwell) Dexter.

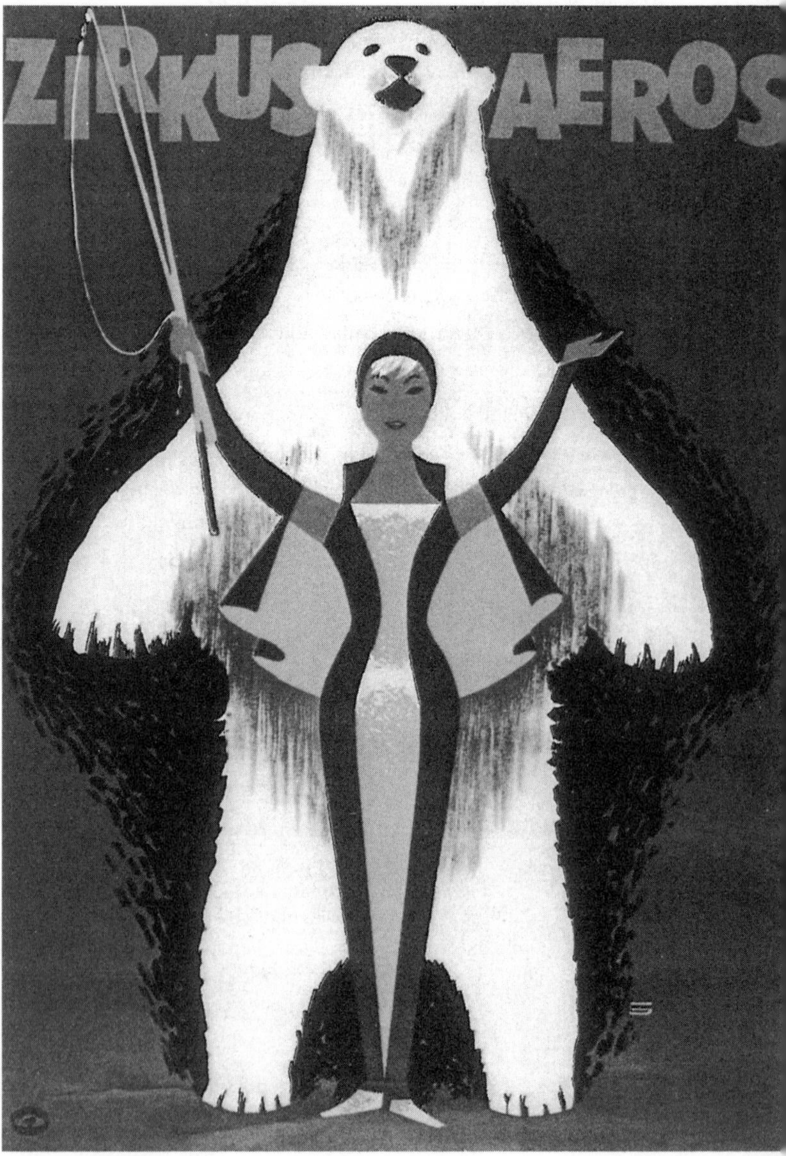
ZIRKUS AEROS

# Bears on Show

When we think of the ways in which humans and bears interact, hunting is probably the first thing that comes to mind. Its techniques have become more sophisticated, but the practice itself has been a constant since time immemorial. Yet beyond hunting lies a whole set of interactions in which bears feed not our bodies, but our imaginations. Performances featuring bears occupy a full spectrum of possibilities, from cruel, blood-drenched spectacle to more playful forms of entertainment. Sometimes humans also play a starring role, while at other times they are kept at a safe distance. As we trace the shared history of humans and bears, we inevitably follow the ways humans have put bears "on show."

Staged fights between animals have been popular since at least Roman times: the tyrant Caligula once pitted four hundred bears against gladiators and dogs in the arena. He was overshadowed, however, by Gordianus, who managed in his twenty-day reign as Caesar to stage a fight with a thousand bears. Voyeurism and cruelty exerted a formidable mass appeal.

Fights among animals were part of popular culture for centuries, especially in England, and the bullfights that still take place in Spain and France give us only a hint of what these contests

Billboard for the East German circus "Aeros," featuring Ursula Böttcher, "The Brilliant Baroness of the Bears" (ca. 1960s).

A bear and his master in Roman times.

may have been like. The bears that played a part in such spectacles were predominantly smaller brown or black bears—as bones unearthed in the vicinity of English arenas prove. Evidence exists that fights involving polar bears also took place, but such larger, more powerful animals posed a far greater danger to the dogs. A list from the London Bear Garden from 1590 mentions nine bears by name, including Jeremy, Danyell, Tom Hunkes, and Harry of Tame. The list from 1638 is even longer and includes George of Cambridge, Don John, Ben Hunt, and Kate of Kent. These animals were extremely valuable, costing more than a craftsman would earn in an entire year.

To stage a balanced contest, the organizers would remove the bear's claws and canine teeth. The animal was furthermore fitted with a nose ring or an iron neck chain to which a rope was attached. This rope could be tied to a wooden post in the middle of the arena, considerably limiting the bear's circle of movement. At this point the dogs, whose job was to try to seize the bear by the throat or snout, were let into the arena. Using all its strength, the bear attempted to fend them off with his paws. If one managed to latch onto the bear, victory was declared for the dogs and an attendant would stop the fight by prying the winner's jaws open with a bar. If the bear was able to hold off the dogs, however, only the current round ended, and the contest would continue with a new set of dogs. Although the bear's death was not the goal, it was not uncommon for a bear to die during a series of such fights.

By the 1500s, centuries had passed since wild bears roamed Britain, but the fights continued to be a profitable business, and no effort or expense was spared to import the animals from other countries, especially Russia. It was only at the end of the eighteenth century that voices were raised in protest against such spectacles. Those who objected were concerned primarily not with cruelty to animals, but rather with moral decline, since, as the Puritan Babington Macaulay explained, the spectators derived a sinfully excessive amount of pleasure from the fights. Eventually the forces of reform won the day: the Society for the Prevention of Cruelty to Animals was founded in England in 1824, and in 1835 an animal-protection law was passed, although its provisions did not extend to wild animals.

Fights between bears and bulls or dogs continued to be a prime attraction in nineteenth-century California. In Pakistan—where such contests became popular during the period of British rule—it is still possible to see bear fights today. Although such contests have been outlawed for more than a century, eyewitnesses report brutal spectacles involving up to a dozen bears and hun-

"The Delights of the Fair" (1877).

dreds of bull terriers. Evidence also exists that bear spectacles may have played a role in the horrors that occurred in Nazi concentration camps: according to a testimonial from Buchenwald survivor Morris Hubert, each day a Jewish prisoner there was thrown into a bear pit and ripped to pieces by the animal held there. Throughout history, bears have played a key role in the enactment of humanity's darkest fantasies—fantasies for which these unwilling actors bear none of the blame.

OF COURSE, BEARS DO NOT have to be violent to entertain us. Over time, humans have taken immense pleasure from not only subduing animals to their will, but also seeing them behave like humans. Why do we find such displays so interesting? Forcing animals to mimic human behavior can be a way for us to express our perceived superiority and inscribe and foster the dividing line between humans and other species. However, such practices may also serve to acknowledge and demonstrate our kinship with them or to resolve the subconscious fear of the underlying similarity we share. While it is hardly fair to the animals, we humans have always used them to define what we are ourselves.

FOR MORE THAN A THOUSAND years people have traveled through Europe with bears who "dance" or otherwise perform for audiences. In southeastern Europe such bear tamers most often were gypsies, who were known for their skill in training not only bears but also apes and dogs. To handle the bear more easily, they would put a ring through the animal's nose and outfit it with a muzzle. According to popular accounts, they treated their charges with a great deal of respect and never killed older animals because they viewed bears as their ancestors.

But is it really possible to train a bear without using violence? Such a feat is very unlikely. Today we know from a number of sources that trainers would teach bears to "dance" by placing them in a structure with an uncomfortably hot floor and then playing drums and other instruments. The bears would stand up and hop quickly from one foot to the other to avoid getting burned. Once conditioned in this way, the animals could be made to "dance" about by the sound of the music alone.

Such practices were not limited to Europe. An eighteenth-century report relates that sloth bears were considered easy to train and were therefore often led about by entertainers. At the beginning of the nineteenth century Thomas Williamson, a British officer of the East India Company, wrote that the bears "are taught to dance, and to understand various phrases to which they make appropriate signs of dissent or approbation, as may suit the occasion. Many are very adroit in making a *salaam,* or obeisance, and show more docility than one would suppose such an heavy animal could possess." But Williamson also warned that "amidst all their acquiescence to the master's will, however, they often betray their natural disposition, and resist every attempt to bring them to subordination. Their tutors sometimes wrestle with them, but this is a mere piece of mummery and ill supports the pretended difficulty which a man has in overcoming a bear."

In the eighteenth and early nineteenth centuries, traveling animal shows followed in the wake of such traditional bear acts. The organizers advertised these spectacles by hanging posters, usually featuring animals that were exotic or at least dangerous, throughout the locality the day before the show. Exhibitors soon learned

Indian miniature painting, nineteenth century.

that they could expect larger audiences if they not only displayed their charges, but also told spectators something about them. Not surprisingly, the stars of these shows were often made out to be more mysterious than they actually were. For example, although the sloth bear was known to be a specific type of bear by 1819, it was still being advertised as a more alluring "unknown Bengalese beast" long after this date. Sim-

"Mores portans des singes et menans des ours." Print by Israël Silvestre and Jacques Bailly, taken from *Grand Caroussel donné à Paris en 1662*. It is not clear whether the bears are real or humans in bearskins.

ilarly, an announcement from 1816 seems to advertise a mythical creature: "A black African Baribal or bastard hyena mix, 6 feet tall, with smooth hair."

Such exaggerations probably inspired the German theologian and writer C. Th. Griesinger to compose a satiric text in 1839 describing the wondrous "North American polar bear, from the Cape of Good Hope." According to Griesinger's tongue-in-cheek account, the animal "was brought down in the depths of Siberia during a cold wave of 175 degrees by traveling Negroes who succeeded in opening one of his veins and who presented him alive to the emperor of Morocco. He builds his den under the snow, which, when the weather turns very cold, he heats with a mixture of turf and black coal. He is a great friend of frozen treats and is therefore also called the 'lip-smacking bear.' During the Russian campaign of 1812 half of his brain froze, and when it

Poster for a menagerie. The polar bear is at the upper right.

Mit Königlicher allerhöchster Bewilligung.

# Große Menagerie

von

merkwürdigen und äußerst schönen fremden Thieren.

is terribly cold he tends to wrap his fur around his body twice at night, but he still doesn't die before his time has come."

Soon bears were expected to do more than just appear in front of an audience or balance on a rolling barrel. After 1830, increasingly complicated tricks appeared on the program. The bears would be given nothing to eat for hours and then presented with pieces of meat during the show. These would then be taken away again so that the trainer could demonstrate the control he had over the animals. Although such animal shows did not enjoy the best reputation, many a zoo operator saw himself as following in the footsteps of "Mr. Menagerist." Alfred Brehm, the director of the Hamburg Zoo, wrote in 1866 that he considered such entrepreneurs to be the zookeeper's "teachers and role models."

Carl Hagenbeck, one of the major European animal dealers of his time, is said to have offered about a thousand bears for sale between 1866 and 1886. "Pity and the conviction that there must be a way into the psyche of this animal" led him to introduce what he called nonviolent training, a method that supposedly transformed the work of animal tamers. But can words and harmless tricks alone really bring animals to do things they would never do in real life? What role do whips, gunshots, and the withholding of food truly play?

The rise of the animal-protection movement brought harsh criticism of the practice of bear taming. One such voice belonged to the animal-rights activist Emil Knodt, who in 1912 wrote a fictitious autobiography of a dancing bear to draw attention to the plight of such animals: "When humans are happy, they dance, but when bears dance they are anything but happy," Knodt's protagonist laments. "For the past five years I have traveled through all the countries under the sun, from the North to the South and from the East to the West. . . . My master often hits me when I am tired and can't dance properly any more. He earns his bread through my effort alone and he should at least be gentle and good to me."

At the end of the nineteenth century the American circus veteran George Conklin championed the view that, while only punishment could bring lions to perform, bears would respond to words alone. Bears, he claimed, possess understanding and a remarkable talent for learning. Animal tamers thus trained bears with pointed sticks, which they used to bring the animals into the positions desired. Getting bears to pedal when learning to ride bicycles proved to be particularly difficult. The trainer would tickle the sole of the performer's paw until the bear would raise it into the air. Balancing on balls, seesaws, and tightropes and riding motorcycles and bicycles all became part of the repertoire of the "com-

Polar bear spectacular (ca. 1900).

ical teddy-bear schools." Daring performers such as Jean Baptiste Pezon or Fred Seylon would even wrestle with bears.

The list of bear attractions continued well into the twentieth century, and by then such spectacles had to entertain large, demanding crowds: Willy Hagenbeck, Carl's nephew, boasted a troupe of seventy polar bears. Willy Hagenbeck moved his ferocious charges about as easily as a shepherd would herd his sheep. The animals could build "decorative pyramids" and ended each performance with a "comical water slide." This trainer's claim to fame was that he could wield a whip—which for the animal represents an extension of the trainer's arm—equally well with either hand and could strike the spot he was aiming for within an inch. We also know that he used so-called hand grenades—roughly carved wooden truncheons that he always had at the ready. As soon as a bear misbehaved, the trainer would call the animal's name loudly and harshly. At the same moment, a blow with the truncheon would underscore the reprimand by striking the wrongdoer in such a way that the animal could not determine where the blow had originated. Willy Hagenbeck also used a large wooden fork to fend off the bears when they lost their patience with this treatment.

The bears under the direction of the female trainer Cate Pallenberg, frequent performers in America and guests at Berlin's famous Wintergarten in 1926, drove the anthropomorphism of such shows to previously unknown heights:

they roller-skated, drove a car, walked on stilts, danced, played the drums, and even rowed a boat. And the daring performance of Munich's Lilo Schäfer formed a high point of Jack Hylton's London circus during the 1950s: the lovely bear trainer, dressed as an ice princess in a blue fur costume with a white satin lining, would step into a cage full of savage polar bears. The following decade Ursula Böttcher toured in the United States, France, Spain, and Japan with a troupe of polar bears and was soon nicknamed "Brilliant Baroness of the Bears." Originally from Leipzig in East Germany, and measuring a little more than five feet tall, she was an employee of the East German state and brought home record earnings. The "death kiss" that Böttcher would give to her bears is legendary.

The obviously involuntary character of the star performers' participation prompted advocates of animal taming to justify the practice. Back in the 1930s, zoologist E. Kuckuck classified dancing, jumping through tires, and balancing on barrels as "natural" tricks, claiming that rewards alone, such as food, could bring the animals to perform them. Twenty years later, in the 1950s, Swiss animal psychologist Heini Hediger asserted that learning such tricks contributed to the psychological well-being of animals and was a source of "enjoyment" for them. For Hediger, tricks could serve as "meaningful" activities for animals kept in zoos. At least he reserved this positive judgment for those tricks that cleverly exploit the bear's natural flight reaction and other reflexes, such as prompting the animal to climb onto a swing, clamber over a pyramid, or the like. Hediger decidedly condemned acts such as riding motorcycles as "kitsch."

It was commonly believed that, as long as they were treated well, polar bears would remain harmless and obedient as they grew older. As far as we know, this was indeed true for the animals in Hermann van Ufen's menagerie during the first half of the twentieth century. Accounts relate that the trainer would go to a venerable "grandfa- ther" bear in his cage, hug and stroke it, allow it to take a piece of sugar from his mouth, or move it into all kinds of positions. Van Ufen was said to have particularly enjoyed it when the polar bear would sit up on its hind legs, creating a kind of "easy chair." He would then make himself com- fortable on the bear's knees and lean back against its stomach.

The tragic accident that befell Adolf Cossmy (born "Kossmeyer") in the mid-1930s, however, shows that handling large predators, however trusted and seemingly "tame," can still be a lethal undertaking. Cossmy, who as a young man had traveled the world with groups of bears and lions, often approached his bears "naked"—that is, without a whip and fork. His favorite animal was a large polar bear that sometimes posed as a model for artists. Cossmy had the unusual habit of giving the bear a kiss whenever its work was completed. Ironically enough, this be- loved bear would be the end of him. One

Alfred Cossmy kissing his bear.

"Where's the bear?"

morning, as he was lathering and scrubbing the animal, he stumbled over an empty can, whereupon the startled bear flung himself upon its trainer and killed him.

When the Norwegian explorer Roald Amundsen proposed the idea of using polar bears to pull the sleds for an Arctic expedition, Carl Hagenbeck, with the assistance of animal trainer Reuben Castang, set about preparing twenty-one polar bears for the job. It supposedly took nine weeks for the bears, working in small groups, to learn to pull the sleds. But this remarkable plan ultimately went unfulfilled: when Amundsen failed to persuade Reuben Castang to accompany him to the polar regions, he decided against using "sled bears" after all.

BESIDES CIRCUSES, ZOOS have provided the most important "stage" for displaying bears. Zoos are so common today that we tend to take them for granted, but like any cultural institution they are the products of complex historical developments. While the first real zoos are a product of the nineteenth century, we might trace their beginnings back to ancient Rome, where bears were held in pits or trenches. One of the most famous bear enclosures, however, was the bear pit built at the end of the fifteenth century in the Swiss capital of Bern. Observers, their gaze directed downward, could gape at the bears from a safe distance. Although a bear master was always present, it did not take long for the first accident to occur: in 1582 a child fell into the pit and was slightly wounded by two young bears. On numerous occasions bears escaped from the pit and terrorized the city's inhabitants before being summarily shot. The first human fatality occurred in 1861, when a drunken Norwegian captain did a flip on the railing and plummeted into the pit. Three additional casualties have also been documented.

The French occupation of Bern in 1798 brought dramatic consequences for that city's bears. The three animals living in the pit were "packed" into crates reinforced with copper bands and brought to Paris on three wagons pulled by six horses each. When the weary travelers finally arrived at their destination they refused for hours to leave the crates. Eventually a live duck was used to lure them into the

"Misfortune in the Bear Pit."

The Elector of Saxony's bear garden (seventeenth century).

menagerie in the Jardin des Plantes. For a short time thereafter, the empty bear pit was used to house inmates from Bern's prison.

The impressive and often luxuriously decorated bear houses that appeared in city zoos in the nineteenth century marked the end of the popularity of bear pits. It is tempting to view these new constructions as evidence of a change in the public's attitude toward bears, since spectators no longer looked down at the animals from above but rather saw them eye to eye. Enclosures that offered the bears more opportunities to move about or retreat from view were first built at the end of the nineteenth century. A complex that included a pool and a cliff wall with an artificial cave was built at this time at New York's Central Park Zoo and was considered a model

bear habitat. However, these improved lodgings could not prevent a common problem in zoos: all too often, mother bears would pay little attention to their young or, worse, eat them. Promptly deploying a dog to serve as foster mother could help to avoid the worst.

Bear house in the Frankfurt Zoological Garden (late nineteenth century).

In the meantime, zoo bears have come to be considered individuals. They often have names, and their health and reproductive behavior is closely followed by the press. The pandas—the "stars" among the bears—can command the public's undivided attention. In the National Zoo in Washington, D.C., where the giant pandas Mei Xiang and Tian Tian are on loan from the China Wildlife Conservation Association, even the shipping crates in which the bears traveled to

Der braune u. schwarze Bär.

From *Robinson's*
*Thierbude*
(Robinson's
Animal
Collection)
(1856).

the United States are on display, along with some of the letters the animals have received from admirers.

ONE ADDITIONAL INSTITUTION deserves our attention—although in this case the bears on show were in no position to notice their position on center stage. Natural history museums displaying taxidermic specimens became popular in the second half of the nineteenth century, and bears have always been among their most popular attractions. It would be illusory to imagine that the animals exhibited there experienced natural deaths, as if they had been discovered preserved

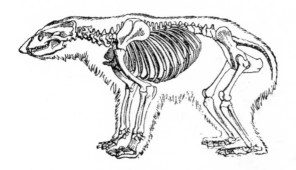

by the Siberian cold after peacefully dying in their sleep. Occasionally animals that had died in zoos were used, but often the specimens were hunted and killed for this purpose alone. During his four-year journey in northern Canada (1908–12) Vilhjalmur Steffansson wrote that "I encountered a gray bear that I had to shoot because the animal researcher wanted him so badly and one

Bear "family" in a museum in Sapporo, Japan (ca. 1930).

Stuffed Kodiak bear on display.

of the main purposes of the trip was acquiring these rare museum pieces." The demand was great: at the turn of the twentieth century, about 250 natural history museums existed in both Great Britain and the United States, another 300 in France, and 150 in Germany.

At first the skins were simply stuffed with straw or cotton, but later a process using so-called dermoplastic was perfected. The goal was to present the animals in "lifelike" poses, ideally in movement. Philipp Leopold Martin, who deepened his zoological knowledge on trips to eastern Europe and South America before joining the Zoological Museum in Berlin, regularly criticized the practice of simply "skewering" the specimens on wires. Instead, he worked from sketches of living animals. Starting with a two-dimensional wooden form that represented a side view of the body, Martin developed a three-dimensional profile of wood and wire, which he then wrapped in linen. The resulting mummies were displayed alone or in impressive group poses in glass cases. We also have Martin to thank for the idea of displaying predators along with their prey.

The final touch was to create artificially lit dioramas so that museum visitors could enjoy the sensation of strolling through a forest, desert, steppe, or polar landscape. Sometimes animals were even placed in the middle of the museum's open areas. The human nuclear family served as a popular model for these displays, prompting scenes featuring Papa, Mama, and Baby Bear together—a pleasing sight, to be sure, but one no more realistic than the story of Goldilocks.

AS OUR ATTITUDES TOWARD animals have changed, so have the ways we look at entertainment in which they play a part. Circuses that feature bears and other wild animals face severe criticism today. Many animal-rights activists consider circus bears to be enslaved creatures and their training regime to be little more than animal cruelty; a circus, they argue, does not offer appropriate conditions for holding wild animals. Such activists may tear down circus posters or post animal-rights stickers on them. This controversy raises the question: should acts involving performing bears, elephants, and monkeys be outlawed, or do stricter regulations promise an adequate solution? "Without animals, the traditional circus is dead," claimed Martin Hanson, the Danish president of the European Circus Association. Hanson noted that menageries stopped featuring dancing bears years ago and pointed out that existing laws forbid presenting animals in ways that could lead to injury or pain. Of course, many of us harbor fond childhood memories of visits to the circus and the amusing and amazing animals we saw there. But as we learn more about bears, our perceptions and ways of dealing with them must change.

For many observers, a trip to the zoo likewise

raises many questions. Why do zoo animals often have human names? What do we actually learn about bears when we see one in a zoo? Do we really get an impression of anything more than the animal's physical appearance and a few of its elementary movements? How has life in such close quarters affected the behavior of these animals? Zoos have come under criticism lately for a number of reasons that are hard to ignore. One issue is the fact that zoos, by definition, create artificial worlds that tell visitors little about the natural environments of the animals kept in them. Bob Mullan and Garry Marvin take this argument a step further by insisting that "the presentation of captive wild animals in the zoo reveals more about the human societies which have constructed them—and whose members roam freely through them—than about the animals which are confined within them."

A more serious problem than zoos' questionable educational value is the living conditions for animals there. While for some small animals the difference between living in a zoo or the wild may not be all that great, it is unlikely that an animal like a polar bear finds zoo life ideal. Each of us has probably witnessed the compulsive movements of certain animals in zoos that, day after day, pace the same number of steps back and forth, swim repetitive figure eights, or swing their heads up and down while stamping their front paws. The animals hardly behave this way because they enjoy such repetitive movements, as these are not normal behavioral patterns. Instead, they are likely compensating for their thwarted desire to flee. Drug therapy is one common approach to this problem. However, there have been successful attempts to improve captive environments and alter the design of zoos. For example, Hal Markowitz of San Francisco State University has constructed complex pieces of equipment that get bears to work harder to earn their food and to do other things that are more normal and interesting to them.

Consider the polar bear's behavior in the wild: when *Ursus maritimus* runs, it can easily reach a speed of twenty-five miles per hour. Instead of having a fixed territory, polar bears are constantly on the move, following the edge of the polar ice cap south in the winter and north again in the summer. It is not unusual for a bear to cover fifty miles a day in the course of its travels. Some behavioral scientists thus object to keeping polar bears in zoos because captivity results in stress, frustration, and behavioral changes such as pacing and neglecting their young. According to Georgia Mason, a behavioral biologist, there is a correlation between the size of an animal's natural territory and its infant mortality rate in zoos. In a series of studies, she has calculated that the smallest polar bear territory in the wild is still about a million times larger than an average zoo enclosure. Zoos that keep bears despite these discrepancies claim that they help to ensure the survival of endangered species or that the bear's territories are so large in the wild only because available prey is scarce.

THE EASE AND AFFORDABILITY of long-distance travel means that today we do not have to be satisfied with seeing bears in the zoo, but can observe them in their natural habitat. A whole business has developed around this practice. "Bear watching" from cars or airplanes is immensely popular and seems like a win-win situation: it can help increase public support for bear conservation and does not involve confining the animals in an artificial space. Yet observing bears in the wild is fraught with complications. The International Association for Bear Research and Management (IBA) has pointed out that prying human eyes can disturb the very animals that tourists want to see in the first place and even alter the bears' behavior in subtle but detrimental ways. The presence of humans and their vehicles may cause bears to abandon preferred habitats, and it may force them to leave their dens earlier than they otherwise would, lead to early separation of mothers from their cubs, and contribute to increased vigilance on the part of the animals—with consequences for bear survival, reproductive success, and conservation. We have to keep in mind that any human intrusion—including researchers who want to help the bears—can have negative effects, so it is always necessary to weigh the pros and cons of such actions. Televised images of individuals approaching bears too closely can suggest that such proximity is safe and might encourage viewers to try the same. The IBA therefore urges reporters covering stories involving humans and bears to remember that the media can influence public perception and behavior and to seek the perspective of wildlife agencies.

# CHAPTER FIFTEEN

# Bear Substitutes

What most people in Europe in the nineteenth century knew about bears came from old fairy tales and fables. Although the images of bears that these stories offer have little in common with the real animal, they nonetheless shaped how people imagined bears to be. Fables—most of which probably originated with the Greek writer Aesop (6 B.C.)—use animals to give a moralizing lesson. In such tales, Bruin the bear often serves as a counterpart to the clever and wily fox by playing the part of the naïve dupe. For example, in one story Reynard the fox persuades a bear to try ice fishing. The poor bear freezes fast to the ice and loses his tail in his efforts to free himself—an often-used explanation as to why the bear's tail is so short.

The bear cuts an equally dim-witted figure in the well-known fable of the bear and the gardener. In this story, a gardener who lived alone was looking for a companion and came across a friendly bear, who proceeded to become the protector of his new friend. One afternoon the gardener fell asleep and the faithful bear remained awake to shoo the flies from his face. One of the flies proved to be persistent, and the bear, at the end of his patience, decided to hit it with a large rock . . . thereby breaking two of the gardener's

Shirley Temple and her beloved Teddy Bear.

The bear and the gardener.

front teeth. Like most fables, this little story teaches us a valuable lesson: it is better to have prudent enemies than ignorant friends. During the Renaissance, famous writers such as Jean de Lafontaine (1621–1695) reworked such ancient fables into delightful literary stories, helping to ensure that the images of bears these stories offer continued to influence the attitude of later generations.

Fairy tales, which we tend to know better today than fables, reveal a change in how humans saw bears. In "Snow White and Rose Red," one of the fairy tales the Grimm brothers collected in the nineteenth century, a widow invites a passing bear to come into her house and warm himself by the fire. The ursine visitor stays the whole winter and rescues the widow's lovely daughters, Snow White and Rose Red, from a wicked dwarf who threatens their lives. At the moment the bear kills his foe, he turns into the requisite handsome prince. The now hunky rescuer explains that the dwarf had put a spell on him and marries the comely Snow White. (Rose Red, in turn, ends up with the prince's brother, who conveniently appears at the close of the story.)

This remarkable denouement represents a revolution in our view of bears: not only does it seem to evoke the ancient cultural bond between our species, but it also foreshadows and accompanies the profound shift in how bears would be perceived in the decades to come. This new attitude may have to do with the realization that bears had disappeared from vast stretches of the earth, making the animals something threatened and precious. It is tempting to read the story as symbolizing a longing to reinstitute a deeper connection between humans and bears. In other nineteenth-century children's books, bears appear in various human roles, although now they are sometimes portrayed as lonely and thoughtful, or even as acting as teachers or kings of the forest. Not surprisingly, given the human characteristics attributed to them, they are shown walking upright in almost every case.

In 1894, Baloo entered the picture. The famous bear from Rudyard Kipling's *Jungle Book* befriends Mowgli, a young boy kidnapped by the tiger Sher Khan and left in the jungle. With the help of Baloo and a black panther named Bagheera,

Mowgli comes of age in this hostile environment. The drawings that Kipling's father prepared of Baloo show an animal closely based on its real-life models. But the Baloo most of us know—the one in Walt Disney's animated feature of 1967—has evolved significantly from these more or less realistic beginnings: ungainly and not terribly bright, he is an easygoing fellow who takes things as they come and doesn't let anything upset him.

The bear as the king of the forest. From a children's book by Franz Wiedemann (1884).

During the decadent fin de siècle, bears were all the rage: stuffed bears dispensed cigars or held ashtrays at the ready, life-size bear figures of wood or metal served as hat stands, and bearskins provided exotic rugs on which naked beauties could sprawl. Sometimes the skins—complete with paws—were even used to fashion bulky, remarkably ugly "bear chairs." Bears were also a popular motif for artists at the turn of the century. One picture from about 1903 shows two women standing at a bear pit and throwing rose petals to the bear below. In Munich artist Leo Putz's *Bacchanale,* which created a scandal at the Munich Art Exhibition, nude women are shown "wrestling" with a polar bear and a brown bear, as well as with a black panther, a leopard, and a lion. Interestingly, the defenders of morality objected to the depiction of licentious women but not to the connotations of eroticism between humans and animals. Another Putz painting offers a less explicit treatment of the same theme: a masked woman performs a dance with a bear.

Minor revolutions were also occurring in the toy industry. Mechanical bears covered with fur or leather, mostly manufactured in France, had been on the market since the 1880s. By the turn of the century, these and other such toys had reached an astounding level of complexity. In a 1904 book, teacher Paul Hildebrandt described a number of these automated playthings: charming puppies that run in circles, wagging their heads from side to side; goats that approach, bleating complainingly; and roaring and gesturing bears that dance, drink, and even smoke. One of the most remarkable toys in Hildebrandt's account is a dollhouselike laundry that would put most modern toys to shame. Seven white cats wash, boil, rinse, and scrub away to a music-box

The bear as a hermit.

Mowgli and the bear used to look quite different.

*Dance with Bear,*
by Leo Putz
(1869–1940).

tune until an unwelcome visitor arrives. "Then—what a fright—the door opens, and a bear dressed as a chimney sweep appears," Hildebrandt recounted. "But a clever kitty closes the door again, and the monster must stay outside."

It is difficult to avoid the impression that bears had to first disappear from the forests before we could perceive them through a lens of such lovable harmlessness. But this view of bears was on its way to becoming an indelible part of many childhoods when Richard Steiff, nephew of the doll maker Margarete Steiff, designed a toy bear with fur made of shaggy mohair, identified as "PB55." The Steiff company—which still sells the beloved stuffed animals sporting buttons on their ears today—presented the new plaything at the Leipzig Toy Show in the spring of 1903. At first the bear met with little interest, but then New York businessman Hermann Berg submitted an order for three thousand of the toys. Another twelve thousand were sold that same year. Berg, a toy buyer for the wholesaler Borgfeldt & Co., had a reason to take interest in PB55—he had witnessed the birth of the teddy bear in America half a year earlier, on November 16, 1902. On that momentous day, the *Washington Post* published a cartoon that inspired Brooklyn store owners Rose and Morris Michtom to create a new product. The cartoon showed President Theodore Roosevelt, a passionate bear hunter, facing a second hunter holding a small bear. Roosevelt objects to shooting the bear, claiming that he would no longer be able to look his children in the eye if he were to kill such a defenseless creature.

"Don't shoot this bear!"

That very day the Michtoms fashioned a toy bear from cloth, stuffed it with sawdust, and gave it boot buttons for eyes. They wrote "Teddy's Bear" on a small sign and put their creation in the shop window along with the newspaper clipping. In only a short time, the story goes, twelve different people had expressed interest in buying the toy. The couple also sent a bear to Roosevelt, who agreed that they could call it "Teddy." And while the Michtoms' idea was soon copied by many other toy manufacturers, Teddy paid off handsomely for his inventors. They soon founded the Ideal Novelty and Toy Company, which their family owned until the 1970s.

The original stuffed bears bore a relatively close resemblance to their counterparts in the animal kingdom, but over the course of the past century the majority of such toys came to look less and less like their real-life models. Their faces have grown flatter, their eyes larger, and their legs shorter, and they often sport pink or baby-blue fur and rounded potbellies. These are bears the

Theodore Roosevelt, the hunter.

way people love them: harmless companions we can cuddle with or take along as companions—like Sebastian Flyte in Evelyn Waugh's *Brideshead Revisited,* who drove through the English landscape with "Aloysius" in the passenger seat. For many if not most people, bears are thus among the first animals they are aware of as children, even if in a harmless and manageable form. The teddy bear wave soon ushered in a series of humanoid bears in books and cartoons. Rupert Bear, Winnie the Pooh, the Berenstain Bears, and Yogi Bear are only a few examples.

But why are teddy bears so popular in the first place? Sergius Golowin wrote that teddies found themselves on the way to becoming "symbols 'of youth at every age' in a contemporary mythology." The faces of bear cubs and the toy bears based on them correspond ideally to the model that the famous behavioral researcher Konrad Lorenz described in the 1940s. Lorenz argued that the facial characteristics typical of small children trigger a protective reflex in humans, a reaction that, from a biological perspective, helps to ensure the survival of the species. Although this theory was of course unknown to toy manufacturers at the beginning of the twentieth century, they still sensed that the generalized representation of a diminutive, toothless bear with a snub nose, fat cheeks, small ears, and a cuddly, rounded body beneath its fur possesses all the traits that awaken sympathy in humans and motivate them to buy. For adults, teddy bears can provide a means to imagine ourselves back to our childhoods. Giving

a teddy bear to one's sweetheart even has romantic connotations, as Golowin confirmed when he classified such a gift as a sign for an approaching engagement, marriage, or partnership.

French cultural anthropologist Jean-Dominique Lajoux, in turn, views teddy bears as a continuation of an age-old custom. In the past, a piece of real bear fur or a bear paw—or sometimes a rabbit's foot, which is still considered a lucky charm today—would be hung as a talisman or fetish on the beds of young children. Because their thick fur hides the male's sex organs, and because bears do not necessarily have to eat meat, they can seem harmless, a fact that may also contribute to their popularity as toys. An animal that, at least superficially, does not seem all that animalistic can easily be adapted for our own purposes. But bears have left their traces on the pleasurable pursuits of adults as well: at the beginning of the twentieth century, a series of new American ballroom dances became the rage. These dances, which abandoned the stiff formality of earlier social dance forms, included not only the "fox trot" and the "bunny hug," but also the "grizzly bear." To perform this last dance, the woman wrapped herself tightly around her partner—a display of intimacy that prompted an outcry among the guardians of morality and caused many a ballroom to be summarily cleared.

The once-popular dance "the bear step"/"Le pas de l'ours," by G. Dantoine (1930).

# Wild West WEEKLY

## A MAGAZINE CONTAINING STORIES. SKETCHES Etc. OF WESTERN

*Issued Weekly—By Subscription $2.50 per Year.   Copyright, 1908, by Frank Tousey, Publisher, 24 Union Square, New York.*

No. 310.        NEW YORK, SEPTEMBER 25, 1908.        Price 5

# YOUNG WILD WEST'S HUNT IN THE HILLS
## OR, ARIETTA AND THE AZTEC JEWELS.
### By AN OLD SCOUT.

As the bear arose and started toward Arietta a cry of warning escaped Wild.  Raising his
he fired at the beast, and it fell with a ball in its brain.  Both Chinamen were
frantic with fear.  "That settles him, Et!" laughed Wild.

# CHAPTER SIXTEEN

# "Bearanoia"

Many if not most humans in the world today no longer understand what it means to live with bears. When a bear does risk proximity to humans, its presence is often interpreted either as a threat to life and property or as a sensation—or both. People, especially in highly developed and densely populated areas, may react to bears in their midst with an excessive, irrational fear that amounts to veritable "bearanoia." Japan offers a poignant example. We would normally expect that, to avert danger to man and beast alike, the driver of a full bus would hit the brakes if he saw a bear on the road. But in May 1958 near Furano-cho, something very different occurred: the driver sped up—and the passengers encouraged him to do it. The poor bear was forced over a cliff and plummeted to its death.

An isolated tragedy? Unfortunately not: historically, Japanese culture has classified the animals as monsters that must be relentlessly hunted. But that's only one side of the coin, because at the same time the bear is honored in Japan as "the king of the beasts," or "the ruler of the forest," as the British cultural anthropologist John Knight discovered in a wide-ranging study of Japanese attitudes toward this animal. The bear there is

Bear encounter on the American frontier, from *Wild West Weekly* (New York), dated September 25, 1908.

寛永元暦の四國合戦を比較なせしが
名を顕し四天王の二人と稱せられる應
臣の美和と代々ふつくり
繪傳略傳史
柳下亭棲員筆記

known as "terrifying demon" *(kyôfu no oni),* and "thief" *(dorobô),* but it also has the more affectionate nicknames "mountain man" *(yamaotoko),* "mountain uncle" *(yama no ossan),* "mountain father" *(yamaoyaji),* and "Mr. Bear" *(kumachan).* A number of men's given names, such as Kumaichi, Kumaji, or Kumao, even include the Japanese character for "bear," and tradition holds that it was bears who discovered several of the hot mountain springs that are now popular tourist attractions.

The bear's demonic image in Japan is not entirely unfounded. A particularly terrible incident took place on the island of Hokkaido in 1915. A 750-pound bear entered the town of Tomomae and over a period of two days killed seven people and seriously wounded three more. When hunters succeeded in bringing the animal down, they celebrated their feat like a military triumph. More than fifty years later, in 1966, the island underwent another round of bear panic. An army of 148 hunters, assisted by 260 others, were outfitted with fifty automotive vehicles, five snowmobiles, and four helicopters and killed a total of thirty-nine bears.

According to Knight, bears have repeatedly forced their way into populated regions of Japan over the past several decades. They have plundered fruit plantations and have eaten the offerings left for the departed in cemeteries. They have even smashed windows to gain entry into houses. A Japanese housewife—so the story

(overleaf)
Fight with a bear,
by Utagawa
Kuniyoshi
(1798–1861).

goes—even found a bear sitting in her living room in front of the television. Residents of places frequented by bears keep the animals at bay with watchdogs, mannequins set up as bear "scarecrows," or unpleasant-smelling substances. Since forests are still being cleared to make way for evergreen farms, and golf courses and ski areas are steadily encroaching on the bears' traditional territory, the situation is not likely to improve.

But there is a glimmer of hope: Japanese biologists have warned that, since the presence of bears is an indicator of the overall health of nature, the animals should be protected. Several nongovernmental organizations are focusing on brown bears on Hokkaido today. Members of the Brown Bear Society, for example, not only host a forum every year to raise public awareness of the need to protect bears, but also set up electric fences, install bear-proof garbage bins, clear bushes along the road to lessen the chance of sudden encounters, and develop educational videos for children.

In the eastern United States, the long-absent black bear is making a comeback. For example, in 1970 only about one hundred bears remained in New Jersey, a number that increased to nearly fifteen hundred by 2003. At the same time, the state's human population nearly doubled between 1950 and 2000, reaching 8.4 million people. Now a large number of human inhabitants unaccustomed to living near such potentially dangerous animals share New Jersey with bears living in a greatly reduced, fragmented habitat, where sources of food fluctuate every year.

Although bears originally inhabited forested regions in the northern and central part of the state, their range has steadily expanded southward and eastward, so that black bears tend to show up more and more frequently in densely populated areas. The results can range from minor annoyances—people find the garbage ripped to shreds or a birdfeeder knocked to the ground —to genuine causes for concern such as bears entering people's homes or attacking them. Local, state, and federal agencies are responding with trap and release programs, limited hunting, and efforts to drive the bears away with rubber bullets and dogs. Hunting may not be the most effective tool, however. Conflicts between people and bears don't occur in the wild but rather where people live—precisely the areas where shooting firearms is neither advisable nor permitted. Such a situation also raises ethical concerns. As the Humane Society of the United States puts it, "Hunting bears to reduce human-bear conflicts is like shooting into a crowd of people to reduce crime." Fortunately, other options exist. Common sense plays a large role—human food and garbage have to be stored out of reach of bears. In agricultural areas, electric fences have been very effective at keeping bears and people out of each other's way. Immunocontraception or fertility control may also help to keep the bear population at manageable levels.

My own country, Germany, provides one of the best examples of modern-day bearanoia. For a few months in 2006, a bear roamed freely through the Bavarian mountains—for the first time in 171 years. Before "Bruno"—as he was quickly dubbed—arrived on the scene, bears survived in the region only in the local legends, or as figures decorating the village fountains or a few old families' coats of arms.

Bruno found his way to Germany from an area in the Italian Alps where, between 1999 and 2002, wildlife preservationists had released ten bears brought from Slovenia. Since that time, these bears have produced at least eleven cubs, including Bruno himself. The young bear had already made a name for himself in his Italian homeland by destroying chicken coops and beehives and attacking rabbits and sheep. At one point specialists had to shoot at him with rubber bullets to keep him from returning to an area where he had already caused damage. Bruno, or, officially, "JJ1" (his parents were called Jose and Jurka), seemed to have little fear of people and repeatedly entered areas near human communities, both in Bavaria and over the border in neighboring Austria, where he left a trail of deer, sheep, and goat carcasses in his wake. Specialists from Finland were brought in to try to capture the bear alive. The group and their dogs, unaccustomed to the heat, became exhausted and returned to the far north just a few days later, and voices began to demand that the government call open season on the ursine "pioneer."

Occasionally glimpsed by humans, Bruno seemed to be nowhere and everywhere—appearing and disappearing like a phantom. A truck driver claimed that he had seen the bear clambering over a highway median. Three mountain bikers glimpsed him near a lake. An animal trainer suggested using a female bear in heat to lure Bruno into a trap—a plan that, since Bruno was not yet sexually mature, was unlikely to succeed. Because of his atypical behavior, politicians feared that the two-year-old bear could easily become a danger to humans, and he earned the label "problem bear." The public's reaction revealed uneasiness: although people were touched by the story, and made jokes about the bear, they were also afraid. Bruno became the star of the summer. Experienced hunters and policemen were put on call.

An authorized hunter eventually killed the bear, sparking public outrage. Shouldn't it have been possible, people insisted, to transport Bruno back into more remote mountain valleys? Couldn't the hunters have tranquilized him rather than kill him? The debate grew and eventually took on diplomatic dimensions when Italy demanded that Germany return the dead bear's body. But Bruno's untimely death did draw attention to the issue of how and if bears should be reintroduced to Germany. Hopefully, answers will be found soon: experts already predict that other bears are likely to cross the border into Bavaria.

Generally, the more harm bears do to livestock, the more that negative attitudes toward them are likely to increase. In Slovenia, where a great part of today's bear range is either settled or used by humans, predators killed about two thousand sheep the second half of the 1990s. Farmers there are generally reimbursed by the state for such damage. In an area of Norway close to the Swedish border, in turn, predators had been killing one-fifth of the free-ranging sheep every year, but a three-year project with one herd there succeeded in reducing the number of animals lost to bears to one lamb and a single ewe. The herd was kept in a corral at night during the grazing season, where two livestock guard dogs brought from Poland and Italy protected them. In several documented incidents, the dogs prevented bears from attacking the sheep. During the day, shepherds and regular herd dogs watched over the animals. While the shepherds' salaries certainly make this management system expensive, the effort pays off by minimizing federal compensation for livestock lost to predators.

Efforts to reintroduce bears into areas where they were once common can also raise concerns because of an increase in the number of resulting encounters. There is no general rule to determine whether bringing back bears is a good idea. When farmers and livestock owners heard of plans to release Slovenian bears in the Pyrenees, the mountain range forming the frontier between France and Spain, an uproar ensued. In a demonstration in the northern Spanish city of Huesca in May 2006, protesters carried signs reading, "Bears on the loose, man in danger," and argued that the threat the bears posed to the economy outweighed the potential benefits they could bring. As a result, wildlife agencies in France have chosen a more gradual approach—only about fifteen bears will be released over the next few years. However, to achieve anything near a viable population in the Pyrenees, the fourteen to eighteen bears living there now will ultimately have to be supplemented with another eighty animals. In an attempt to pacify the surge of emotions the bear project unleashed, the French government emphasized that not a single person has been killed by a bear in the Pyrenees in the last 150 years.

BEARS FIND THEMSELVES at the spot where two deep-seated but contradictory human impulses collide: the desire to feel protected from unforeseeable danger and the longing for unspoiled nature. When bears enter our everyday world they remind us of a mode of existence that we mostly have left far behind. For this reason, bear management programs that counter public excitement—or even panic—with information are critical wherever people have problems coexisting with bears. The presence of bears nearby enriches our lives, but it also demands that we consider a number of factors to reduce the friction between our species. But no matter how ambitious, no measures to accommodate bears can succeed without the genuine commitment of the local population to sharing their surroundings with these large predators.

"WELCOME TO THE GREAT FOREST, LITTLE BROTHER."

# Epilogue

Bears are in trouble today in much of the world for a number of reasons. There is no part of the bear's body that humans have not put to use in one way or another. In some cuisines, bear paws are a prized delicacy, and a list of medical uses that have been ascribed to the various other parts of the animal's body is long indeed. Many people still firmly believe that bear bile offers relief from almost any ailment imaginable. While the active ingredient—Urso-deoxycholic acid (UDCA), or, to those in the medical field, simply *urso*—can now be manufactured synthetically, genuine bear bile is still so sought after in extensive regions of Southeast Asia that an entire industry is built around the lucrative business of providing it. On bear farms, especially in Thailand, China, and Vietnam, Malay or "sun bears"—which are known for their habit of sitting in a way that resembles the Buddha—are kept in narrow cages and their gallbladders regularly "tapped" with shunts for bile. This practice is no doubt as painful as it is cruel.

Bears in the wild have it better, but they can't survive just anywhere. A bear habitat must provide a reliable food supply throughout the year

"Welcome to the great forest, little brother." From *The Billy Bang Book* (1928).

233

and enough privacy for the animals to remain undisturbed. Brown and black bears also need places where they can hibernate. In Europe only the mountain forests still meet the bears' needs— provided that hiking trails, rest areas, and the tendency of human visitors to intensively collect berries, pine cones, and nuts do not negatively affect the animals.

In North America, bears are often effectively cut off from one another by highways, spreading suburbs, industrial areas, and farms so that they might as well be living on separate islands. Geneticists fear that this isolation could inhibit the exchange of genetic information critical for their survival. As scientists now know, inbreeding results in not only noticeably similar markings, but also bone deformations and reduced fertility. But the genetic material of bears living in these compromised habitats can circulate only if the bears themselves can reach one another. The organization Y2Y—Yellowstone to Yukon—is trying to make this possible by building wildlife bridges and highway underpasses so that bears and other animals can travel from one preserve to another.

BEARS FACE NOT ONLY human encroachment into their habitats but also poaching and environmental pollution, which has become so pervasive that even the polar bears are affected by it. Yet the greatest threats to bears may be our own perceptions of them. What cultural filters distort how we see bears today? Are they teddies to love, endangered animals to save, or beasts to fear? Many of the qualities earlier generations attributed to bears may seem unfounded and unfathomable to us, but our own prejudices and assumptions can rest on equally shaky ground.

There is hardly a "cute" or a "funny" role that bears have not played for us. Their images advertise every imaginable type of product and adorn the packaging of countless treats. The tendency to project human qualities onto bears is nearly universal, and it's not difficult to understand why. Its strength and at least occasionally upright stance almost inevitably encouraged human beings, at least in the Northern Hemisphere, to view the bear as our own wild alter ego. But this feeling of kinship is a double-edged sword. While our identification with bears can lead us to value them, it stands in the way of a true understanding of what bears are like. And what are they like? Despite the fact that we can now accurately track bears with technologically advanced equipment and can examine their DNA, we can't fully answer this question. One thing, however, is certain—bears are not much like us after all.

Our fascination with bears also makes it difficult for us to recognize that, no matter how familiar their glance and gait may seem, bears are not interested in people. But indifference on their part should not prevent us from feeling admiration, respectful curiosity, and concern for the bears that share our world. I would like to have faith in our ability to devise intelligent ways for humans and bears to coexist—although I hope this book has made it clear that we should also keep a respectful distance from them. Since completely avoiding anthropomorphism may be impossible, perhaps we can think and speak of the bears as our distant relatives in the forest who have their own ways of doing things and simply prefer to keep to themselves. Let us not be disappointed—the bears cannot help it. We can avoid clashes between humans and bears only if we learn to stay out of their way. Anything else is the stuff of dreams!

# Acknowledgments

I am indebted to Regina Beyer, Beate Heine, Annette Kaiser, Ana Tipa, Ulrich Meyer, Eva Schöning, and, most of all, Detlef Feußner, who helped to keep me sane when everything around me had to do with bears. Jean Thomson Black, Jeffrey Schier, Laura Davulis, Matthew Laird, and their colleagues at Yale University Press in New Haven were cherished partners in this transatlantic project. Many thanks also to Kate Pocock, Katie Harris, and Robert Baldock at the London office of Yale University Press. I was lucky that Lori Lantz, my translator, took an interest in this book early on and was the perfect person for discussing all the difficult issues involved in reworking my material for an English-speaking readership. My sincere thanks also to John Marzluff, who evaluated my manuscript and made very helpful recommendations, and to Scott M. Perkins, who found the time to comment on it while working on his dissertation.

SOPHIE BOBBÉ (FRANCE), Ingmar Braun (Switzerland), Martha Dowsley (Canada), David Graber (USA), Stephen Herrero (USA), Michael Hofreiter (Germany), Catherine Knight (New Zealand), John Knight (UK, not related to the former), Peter Lüps (Switzerland), Georgia Mason (Canada), Hans-Joachim Paproth (Germany), Gernot Rabeder (Austria), Shyamala Ratnayeke (USA/ Sri Lanka), Annelore Rieke-Müller (Germany), Wilfried Rosendahl (Germany), George W. Wenzel (Canada), and Koji Yamazaki (Japan) have been there to help with facts that otherwise would have been difficult to obtain.

WRITING A BOOK OF THIS historical and geographical scope would have been impossible without the help of well-equipped libraries and the people who work for them. My thanks to Carola Pohlmann and her many colleagues, who helped me at various stages at the Staatsbibliothek Berlin; and to Sabine Hackethal, Hannelore Landsberg, Nils Hoff, Hans-Ulrich Raake, and Martina Rißberger at Berlin's Natural History Museum. Susan Snyder, Head of Public Services at the Bancroft Library of the University of California at Berkeley, was quick to respond to my questions. My warm thanks also go to the antique booksellers Wolfgang Kohlweyer and Christoph Janik. Without them, finding many of the illustrations from old books and magazines in this book would have been impossible.

FINALLY, I OFFER THE customary release of everyone mentioned from any liability for errors of fact or judgment: those that remain are not their fault.

# Bibliographic Essay

*Chapter One. Tracking the Paths of Bears*

In addition to these eight species of bears, some scientists insist that the Gobi bear of Mongolia should be classified as a separate species. They argue for this distinction because, at an adult weight of only two hundred pounds, the twenty-five remaining Gobi bears are smaller than other brown bears. See "Status and Management of the Gobi Bear in Mongolia," by Thomas McCarthy, in Servheen, Christopher et al., pp. 131–136.

For more on the early classification of the grizzly bear, refer to the wonderful book by Harold McCracken: *The Beast That Walks Like Man. The Story of the Grizzly Bear* (London: Olbourne Press, 1957).

On the concept of subdividing North American brown bears into evolutionary significant units (ESUs) see Lisette P. Waits et al., "Mitochondrial DNA Phylogeography of the North American Brown Bear and Implications for Conservation," *Conservation Biology* 12 (1998): pp. 408–417.

*Chapter Two. Transformations*

For a complex understanding of bears in the world of the Native Americans, I recommend David Rockwell's *Giving Voice to Bear—North American Indian Rituals, Myths, and Images of the Bear* (Niwot: Roberts Rinehart Publishers, 1991).

The legend of the gypsy woman is taken from Michel Praneuf's *L'ours et les hommes dans les traditions européennes,* (Paris: Imago, 1989) p. 71.

*Chapter Three. The Mystery of the Cave Bear*

Björn Kurtén has written a very good book on this topic: *The Cave Bear Story. Life and Death of a Vanished Animal* (New York: Columbia University Press, 1995).

For the detailed account of Hofreiter's analysis mentioned in the latter part of this chapter, see Michael Hofreiter et al., "Sudden Replacement of Cave Bear Mitochondrial DNA in the Late Pleistocene," *Current Biology* 17 (2007): pp. 122–123.

*Chapter Four. False Steps*

In his *Historie of Foure-footed Beastes* from 1607, Edward Topsell provides the most widely available discussion of the animal during this period. Combining travel narratives, classical sources, and anecdotes, Topsell presents us with a wealth of information available at the time, not only on bears, but on many other creatures as well.

For the article on the development of muscle strength: Henry J. Harlow et al., "Muscle Strength in Overwintering Bears," *Nature* 49 (2001): p. 997.

*Chapter Five. Exotic Discoveries*

The report on current numbers of panda bears was published in "Molecular Censusing Doubles Giant Panda Population Estimate in a Key Nature Reserve," *Current Biology* 16 (2006): p. 451.

*Chapter Six. The Bear's Personality*

For the quotes about bears adapting to hunters see: Theodore Roosevelt, *Hunting Trips of a Ranchman* (New York and London: G. P. Putnam's Sons, 1885).

*Chapter Seven. Sounds, Senses, and Signals*

For the mentioned investigation of activity patterns see P. Kaczensky et al., "Activity Patterns of Brown Bears *(Ursus*

*Arctos)* in Slovenia and Croatia." *Journal of Zoology* 269 (2006): p. 474–485.

## Chapter Eight. Bears as Pets

For an examination of the relationship between certain indigenous tribes in the Amazon and monkeys, including human breastfeeding of these animals, see Loretta A. Cormier, *Kinship with Monkeys: The Guajá Foragers of Eastern Amazonia* (New York: Columbia University Press, 2003).

## Chapter Nine. An Observer in Eastern Siberia

This chapter is based on Leopold von Schrenck, *Reisen und Forschungen im Amur-Lande in den Jahren 1854–1856 im Auftrage der Kaiserlichen Akademie der Wissenschaften zu St. Petersburg* (Travels and researches in the Land of the Amur in the years 1854–1854 by order of the Imperial Academy of Sciences in St. Petersburg) (St. Petersburg, 1858).

## Chapter Ten. Face to Face

The report on the two women killed by grizzly bears in 1967 (with a number of further references) is accessible at Kerry A. Gunther, Information Paper BMO-7, "Bears and Menstruating Women" (2002), www.nps.gov. For an account of this incident, see Jack Olsen, *The Night of the Grizzlies* (New York: Putnam Publishing Group, 1969). Olsen calculates the probability of such a double attack as on the order of one in a trillion.

If we look at predators in a global perspective, the picture is altogether different. It is universally agreed that mosquitoes—thanks to the fact that they can transmit diseases while feeding on us—kill more humans than do any other predators worldwide. But how does the picture change when we focus on large animals? The answer depends on where you look. Wherever bears exist, they are among the most dangerous mammalian predators. However, people are also trampled to death by elephants in Kenya, attacked by lions in India (where danger from bears also exists), and bitten by alligators in Florida.

### Chapter Eleven. Hunters and Hunted

For the various hunting rites of Native American tribes, I again recommend David Rockwell's *Giving Voice to Bear—North American Indian Rituals, Myths, and Images of the Bear* (Niwot: Roberts Rinehart Publishers, 1991).

### Chapter Twelve. The Inuit and Polar Bears

For the full-length study, see George W. Wenzel, "Nunavut Inuit and Polar Bear: The Cultural Politics of the Sport Hunt," *Senri Ethnological Studies* 67 (2005): pp. 363–388.

The difficult choices that polar bear conservationists have to face are the subject of, e.g., Clifford Kraus, "Debate on Global Warming Has Polar Bear Hunting in Its Sights," *New York Times,* 27 May 2006.

### Chapter Thirteen. Closer Than Close

My presentation of Grizzly Adams is based on Richard Dillon's *Grizzly Adams—California's Greatest Mountain Man.* For more about Timothy Treadwell see Nick Jans's *The Grizzly Maze. Timothy Treadwell's Fatal Obsession with Alaskan Bears* (New York: Dutton, 2005).

Bears and humans living in proximity and peacefully is a subject that seems to fascinate many. One case in point is Charlie Russell and Mauren Eens, who "abducted" the three cubs "Chico," "Biscuit," and "Rosie" from a Russian zoo in 1997 to bring them to Kamchatka. Supposedly discarding many old misunderstandings about bears and their assumed violence, they describe the bears' development from dependent cubs to independent creatures but often get lost in other issues along the way. Timothy Treadwell's aspirations are treated with some sympathy. The title of their lengthy book is *Grizzly Seasons: Life with the Brown Bears of Kamchatka* (Richmond Hill: Firefly Books, 2003).

## Chapter Fourteen. Bears on Show

I recommend Gerald Carson's book *Men, Beasts, and Gods—A History of Cruelty and Kindness to Animals* (New York: Scribner, 1972) for a discussion of how the animal-rights movement evolved.

For a cultural history of zoos see Eric Baratay and Elisabeth Hardouin-Fugier, *Zoo: A History of Zoological Gardens in the West* (London: Reaktion Books, 2002), and David Hancock's more critical study, *A Different Nature: The Paradoxical World of Zoos and Their Uncertain Future* (Berkeley: University of California Press, 2002).

## Chapter Sixteen. "Bearanoia"

The description of these Japanese incidents is drawn from John Knight's article "Culling Demons—The Problem of Bears in Japan," in his volume *Natural Enemies. People-Wildlife Conflicts in Anthropological Perspective* (London and New York: Routledge, 2000). My thanks to Keijiro Suga for checking the spelling of the various Japanese terms.

## Epilogue

I hope that many readers will get involved and follow up on how the world's bears are doing. Here are some Web sites you may want to investigate: www.bearbiology.com (International Bear Association); www.bear.org (North American Bear Association); www.polarbearsinternational.org; www.y2y.net (Yellowstone to Yukon Conservation Initiative); www.bearden.org (bear taxon advisory Web site of the American Zoo and Aquarium association); www.lcie.org (Large Carnivore Initiative for Europe); www.bearsmart.com (The Get Bear Smart Society); www.freethebears.org.au.

# Selected Bibliography

Alexejenko, J. A. 1963. *Der Bärenkult der Keten (Jenissei-Ostjaken)*. Edited by V. Diószegi. *Glaubenswelt und Folklore der sibirischen Völker.* Budapest.

Aucapitaine, Baron Henri. 1860. "Sur la question de l'existence d'ours dans les montagnes de l'Afrique septentrionale." *Comptes rendus de l'Académie des Sciences.* Vol. 50, pp. 655–656.

Bachofen, Johann Jacob. 1863. *Der Baer in den Religionen des Alterthums.* Basel: Meiri.

Baker, Steve. 2001. *Picturing the Beast. Animals, Identity, and Representation.* Urbana and Chicago: University of Illinois Press.

Baratay, Eric, and Elisabeth Hardouin-Fugier. 2002. *Zoo: A History of Zoological Gardens in the West.* London: Reaktion Books.

Bekoff, Marc (ed.). 2004. *Encyclopedia of Animal Behavior.* Westport, Connecticut, and London: Greenwood Press.

Bethlenfalvy, Ernst. 1937. *Die Tierwelt der Hohen Tatra.* Spisské Podhradie: Printed by Edmund Schustek.

Bieder, Robert E. 2005. *Bear.* London: Reaktion Books.

Bingley, William. 1802. *Animal Biography, Or Popular Zoology: Comprising Authentic Notes of the Economy, Habits of Life, Instincts; and Sagacity, of the Animal Creation.* London.

Boas, Franz. 1888. *The Central Eskimo. Sixth Annual Report of the Bureau of American Ethnology for the Years 1884–1885,* pp. 339–669. Washington, D.C.: The Smithsonian Institution.

Bobbé, Sophie. 2002. *L'ours et le loup. Essai d'anthropologie symbolique*. Paris: Éditions de la Maison des sciences de l'homme, Institut National de la Recherche Agronomique.

Bobbé, Sophie, and Jean-Pierre Raffin. 1997. *L'ABCdaire de l'ours*. Paris: Flammarion.

Bolte, Johannes (ed.). 1930–1933. *Handwörterbuch des Deutschen Märchens*. Berlin und Leipzig: Walter de Gruyter.

Bourguignat, Jules René. 1867. "Note sur un ursus nouveau découvert dans la grande caverne du Thaya." *Annales des Sciences Naturelles*. Vol. 8.

Brander, Michael. 1964. *The Hunting Instinct. The Development of Field Sports over the Ages*. London: Oliver and Boyd.

Brown, Gary. 1993. *Great Bear Almanac*. New York: Lyons and Burford.

Carson, Gerald. 1972. *Men, Beasts and Gods. A History of Cruelty and Kindness to Animals*. New York: Charles Scribner's Sons.

Comte de Buffon, Georges-Louis Leclerc. 1837. *Buffons Sämtliche Werke*. Cologne.

Corbin, George A. 1988. *Native Arts of North America, Africa, and the South Pacific*. New York: Harper and Row.

Daigl, Christoph. 1997. *"All the World Is But a Bear-baiting." Das englische Hetztheater im 16. und 17. Jahrhundert*. Berlin.

Day, David. 1981. *The Doomsday Book of Animals. A Natural History of Vanished Species*. London.

Dekkers, Midas. 2000. *Dearest Pet: On Bestiality*. New York: Verso.

Della Porta, Giovanni Battista. 1586. *De Humana Physiognomia*. Naples.

Diamond, Jared. 1997. *Guns, Germs, and Steel. The Fates of Human Societies*. New York: Vintage.

Dillon, Richard. 1966. *The Legend of Grizzly Adams. California's Greatest Mountain Man*. Reno: University of Nevada Press.

Durant, John and Alice. 1957. *Pictorial History of the American Circus.* New York: A. S. Barnes.

Esper, Johann Friedrich. 1774. *Ausführliche Nachricht von neuentdeckten Zoolithen unbekannter vierfüßiger Thiere.* Nürnberg: Georg Wolfgang Knorrs seel. Erben.

Feldhamer, George A., Bruce C. Thompson, and Joseph A. Chapman (eds.). 2003. *Wild Mammals of North America. Biology, Management, and Economics.* Baltimore and London: The Johns Hopkins University Press.

Frobenius, Leo. 1954. *Kulturgeschichte Afrikas.* Zürich: Phaidon.

Fudge, Erica (ed.). 2004. *Renaissance Beasts. Of Animals, Humans, and Other Wonderful Creatures.* Urbana and Chicago: University of Illinois Press.

Gass, Patrick. 1807. *Journal of the Voyages and Travels of a Corps of Discovery, Under the Command of Capt. Lewis and Capt. Clarke of the Army of the United States.* Pittsburgh: David McKeehan.

Gessner, Conrad. 1563. *Thierbuch.*

Gimbutas, Marija. 1982. *The Goddesses and Gods of Old Europe.* Berkeley: University of California Press.

Godman, John D. 1828. *American Natural History.* Philadelphia: Carey and Lea.

Golowin, Sergius. 1964. *Magische Gegenwart. Forschungsfahrten durch den modernen Aberglauben.* Bern and Munich: Francke.

Grevé, Carl. 1895. "Die geographische Verbreitung der jetzt lebenden Raubthiere." *Verhandlungen der Kaiserlichen Leopoldinisch-Carolinischen Deutschen Akademie der Naturforscher.* Vol. 63. Band, Halle.

Hachet-Souplet, Pierre. 1898. *Die Dressur der Thiere.* Leipzig: Klemm.

Hallowell, A. Irving. 1926. "Bear Ceremonialism in the Northern Hemisphere." *American Anthropologist.* Vol. 28, no. 1.

Hancocks, David. 2002. *A Different Nature: The Paradoxical World of Zoos and Their Uncertain Future.* Berkeley: University of California Press.

Harlow, Henry J., et al. 2001. "Muscle Strength in Over-wintering Bears." *Nature*. Vol. 409, p. 997.

Harper, Francis. 1945. *Extinct and Vanishing Mammals of the Old World*. New York: American Committee for International Wildlife Protection.

Hearne, Samuel. 1795. *A Journey from Prince of Wales's Fort in Hudson's Bay, to the Northern Ocean*. London: A. Strahan and T. Cadell.

Hediger, Heini. 1979. *Beobachtungen zur Tierpsychologie im Zoo und im Zirkus*. Berlin: Henschel.

Herrero, Stephen. 2002. *Bear Attacks: Their Causes and Avoidance*. Guilford, Connecticut: The Lyons Press.

———. 2005. "During 2005 More People Killed by Bears in North America Than in Any Previous Year." *International Bear News*. Vol. 14, no. 4.

Hildebrandt, Paul. 1904. *Das Spielzeug im Leben des Kindes*. Berlin: Söhlke.

Jans, Nick. 2005. *The Grizzly Maze. Timothy Treadwell's Fatal Obsession with Alaskan Bears*. New York: Dutton.

Kaczensky, P., et al. 2006. "Activity Patterns of Brown Bears (Ursus Arctos) in Slovenia and Croatia." *Journal of Zoology*. Vol. 269, pp. 474–85.

Kameda, Masato, et al. 2005. "Human Dimensions of Brown Bear Management in the Oshima Peninsula, Hokkaido, Japan." Informational paper.

Kausch, Matthias G. 1998. *Der Bär. Seine Bedeutung in der zeitgenössischen indianischen Literatur Nordamerikas*. Würzburg: Königshausen und Neumann.

Kilham, Benjamin, and Ed Gray. *Among the Bears. Raising Orphan Cubs in the Wild*. New York: Henry Holt, 2002.

Knight, John (ed.). 2000. *Natural Enemies. People-Wildlife Conflicts in Anthropological Perspective*. London and New York: Routledge.

Knight, John (ed.). 2003. *Waiting for Wolves in Japan. An Anthropological Study of People–Wildlife Relations*. Oxford and New York: Oxford University Press.

Krasheninnikoff, Stepan. 1764. *The History of Kamchatka*

*and the Kurilski Islands with the Countries Adjacent.*
Gloucester.

Krementz, A. 1888. *Der Bär. Ein Beitrag zur Naturgeschichte desselben und zur Jagd auf Bärwild.* Berlin: Baensch.

Kurtén, Björn. 1975. *The Cave Bear Story. Life and Death of a Vanished Animal.* New York: Columbia University Press.

LaHontan, Baron. 1703. *New Voyages to North America.*

Lajoux, Jean-Dominique. 1996. *L'homme et l'ours.* Grenoble: Glénat.

LaRue, Mabel Guinnip. 1927. *The Billy Bang Book.* New York: Macmillan.

Leroi-Gourhan, André. 1980. *Die Religionen der Vorgeschichte. Paläolithikum.* Frankfurt am Main: Suhrkamp.

Lopez, Barry Holstun. 1978. *Of Wolves and Men.* New York: Simon and Schuster.

Linnaeus, Carl. 1811. *A Tour in Lapland.* London: White and Cochrane.

Magnus, Olaus. 1555. *Historia de Gentibus Septentrionalibus* (Description of the Northern Peoples). Rome.

Manlius, Nicolas. 1998. "L'ours brun en Égypte." *Écologie.* Vol. 29, no. 4.

McClellan, Catharine. 1975. *My Old People Say: An Ethnographic Survey of Southern Yukon Territory, Part 1.* Ottawa: National Museums of Canada.

McCracken, Harold. 1957. *The Beast That Walks Like Man. The Story of the Grizzly Bear.* London: Olbourne Press.

Meyer, Stephen M. 2006. *The End of the Wild.* Cambridge, Massachusetts, and London: MIT Press.

Meyer-Holzapfel, Monika. 1957. "Das Verhalten der Bären (Ursidae)." *Handbuch Zoologie.* Vol. 8, no. 10.

Mills, Enos A. 1973. *The Grizzly. Our Greatest Wild Animal.* New York: Ballantine Books. First published 1919.

Miquel, André. 1994. *Les Arabes et l'ours.* Heidelberg: Universitätsverlag C. Winter.

Morris, Ramona and Desmond. 1982. *The Giant Panda.* New York: Penguin.

Mullan, Bob, and Garry Marvin. 1998. *Zoo Culture*. Champaign: University of Illinois Press.

Newton, Michael. 2002. *Savage Girls and Boys. A History of Feral Children*. New York: Picador.

Niethammer, Jochen, and Franz Krapp (eds.). 1993. *Handbuch der Säugetiere Europas*. Wiesbaden: Aula-Verlag.

Nowak, Ronald M. 1999. *Walker's Mammals of the World*. Baltimore and London: The Johns Hopkins University Press.

Oberländer, Karl. 1905. *Im Lande des braunen Bären. Jagd- und Reisebilder aus Rußland*. Neudamm: J. Neumann.

Paproth, Hans-Joachim. 1976. *Studien über das Bärenzeremoniell. Bärenjagdriten und Bärenfeste bei den tungusischen Völkern*. Uppsala: Religionshistoriska institutionen i Uppsala.

Rabeder, Gernot, et al. 2000. *Der Höhlenbär*. Stuttgart: Thorbecke.

Reebs, Stéphan. 2003. "Experiment of the Month." *Natural History*. Vol. 6, p. 16.

Reichenbach, Anton Benedikt. 1835. *Bildergallerie der Thierwelt oder Abbildungen des Interessantesten aus dem Thierreiche*. Leipzig: Gebhardt und Reisland.

Rockwell, David. 1991. *Giving Voice to Bear. North American Indian Rituals, Myths, and Images of the Bear*. Niwot: Roberts Rinehart.

Roosevelt, Theodore. 1885. *Hunting Trips of a Ranchman*. New York and London: G. P. Putnam's Sons.

Rosenmüller, Johann Christian. 1799. *Beschreibung merkwürdiger Höhlen. Ein Beitrag zur physikalischen Geschichte der Erde*. Leipzig: Breitkopf und Härtel.

Sage, Dean, Jr. 1935. "In Quest of the Giant Panda. An Account Describing the Work of the Sage West China Expedition in the Highlands of Szechwan Province, Near the Borders of Tibet." *Natural History*.

Scheitlin, Peter. 1840. *Versuch einer vollständigen Thierseelenkunde*. Stuttgart und Tübingen: Cotta.

Schneider, Karl Max. 1933. "Zur Jugendentwicklung eines Eisbären, II. Aus dem Verhalten: Lage, Bewegung, Saugen, stimmliche Äußerung." *Der Zoologische Garten.* Vol. 12.

Servheen, Christopher, Stephen Herrero, and Bernard Peyton. 1999. *Bears. Status Survey and Conservation Action Plan.* Gland, Switzerland, and Cambridge, United Kingdom: IUCN.

Shepard, Paul and Barry Sanders. 1985. *The Sacred Paw. The Bear in Nature, Myth, and Literature.* New York: Arkana.

Simpson, Jacqueline, and Steve Roud. 2000. *A Dictionary of English Folklore.* Oxford: Oxford University Press.

Snyder, Susan. 2003. *Bear in Mind: The California Grizzly.* Berkeley: Heyday Books.

Stefansson, Vilhjalmur. 1925. *Das Geheimnis der Eskimos. Vier Jahre im nördlichsten Kanada.* Leipzig: Brockhaus Verlag.

Stimpson, George. 1946. *A Book About a Thousand Things.* New York: Harper and Brothers.

Tänzern, Johann. 1734. *Der Dianen hohe und niedere Jagdt-geheimniß.* Leipzig: Weidmann.

Tennent, J. Emerson. 1861. *Sketches of the Natural History of Ceylon.* London: Longman.

Topsell, Edward. 1607. *The Historie of Foure-footed Beastes.* London: William Laggard.

Tschudi, Friedrich von. 1872. *Das Thierleben der Alpenwelt.* Leipzig: Weber.

Volmar, Friedrich August. 1940. *Das Bärenbuch.* Bern: Haupt.

Von Schrenck, Leopold. 1858. *Reisen und Forschungen im Amur-Lande in den Jahren 1854–1856 im Auftrage der Kaiserlichen Akademie der Wissenschaften zu St. Petersburg.* St. Petersburg.

Wenzel, George W. 2005. "Nunavut Inuit and Polar Bear: The Cultural Politics of the Sport Hunt." *Senri Ethnological Studies.* Vol. 67, pp. 363–388.

Williamson, Thomas. 1807. *Oriental Field Sports*. London: William Bulmer.

Wood, John George. 1877. *Nature's Teachings. Human Invention Anticipated by Nature*. London: Daldy, Isbister.

Zell, Theodor. 1911. *Riesen der Tierwelt. Jagdabenteuer und Lebensbilder*. Berlin: Ullstein.

# Index

# Credits

Archive Wolfgang Kohlweyer: 30, 33 (top), 186, 214; Bancroft Library, University of California, Berkeley: 220; Bridgeman Art Library: 219, 222–23; Chicago Historical Society: 112, 130; Gettyimages, Hulton Archive: 109; Museum für Naturkunde, Humboldt-Universität zu Berlin: 2, 148, 149, 203; Northwestern University Library: 18; Staatsbibliothek zu Berlin, Preußischer Kulturbesitz: 90, 124, 140, 144–45, 202; Versailles Bibliothèque Municipale, photography Jean Vigne: 190